√ 6.95
⟍B&T

Menomon

D1267385

YOUR CHILD'S INTELLECT

A Guide to Home–Based
Preschool Education

T. H. Bell

with practical applications by
ARDEN R. THORUM

OLYMPUS
PUBLISHING COMPANY
Salt Lake City

WINGATE COLLEGE LIBRARY
WINGATE, N. C.

73- 159374 Sept. 6, 1976

Copyright © 1972 by Olympus Publishing Company
937 East Ninth South, Salt Lake City, Utah 84102

All rights reserved. No portion of this book
may be reproduced in any form without the
express written permission of the publisher.

Manufactured in the United States of America.

ISBN 0-913420-02-6 (Cloth)
ISBN 0-913420-03-4 (Paper)

1 2 3 4 5 6 7 8 9 0

Contents

57578

Acknowledgments

The author gratefully acknowledges the contributions of such men as the late Commissioner James E. Allen, Jr., U.S. Office of Education (USOE); Secretary Elliot Richardson, Department of Health, Education and Welfare; and Commissioner Sidney P. Marland, Jr., USOE, for their untiring efforts to bring to fruition a program of early childhood education throughout the nation. The potential for success of this book has been greatly enhanced by their work.

Arden R. Thorum, who is skilled in working with preschool children to build awareness, capabilities to learn, and communicative skills, made a substantial contribution to the book through his work on educational toys and through contributing ideas for parent use of ordinary household items as teaching aids. His practical how-to-do-it applications at the end of each chapter will enable the parents to make their own educational toys and are an embellishment to the original manuscript.

The author is indebted to Sybil H. Clays for her invaluable assistance in editing and offering suggestions for improving the content and clarity of the manuscript, and to G. Donald Gale who designed the book and who had final editorial responsibility for its publication.

Appreciation is also expressed to those parents of preschool children residing at University Village at the University of Utah for suggestions offered following a trial use of the manuscript in a pilot test of the book before its publication.

Foreword

During the time Dr. Bell served as Deputy and Acting Commissioner in the U.S. Office of Education (USOE), considerable national attention was being given to the learning problems of children in the primary grades of school. The national "right to read" program, instituted during the tenure of the late Commissioner James E. Allen, Jr., highlighted the concern that educators had for these problems. The Children's Television Workshop (a nonprofit organization funded by USOE and the Carnegie Foundation) was beginning to produce instructional TV programs for the benefit of preschool children in the home.

When Elliot Richardson assumed the title of Secretary of the U.S. Department of Health, Education and Welfare, he gave the right to read effort the attention it needed. He called upon USOE to give higher priority to early childhood education in general and the national right to read project in particular. The program was faltering when Richardson saved it from an untimely death.

When Sidney P. Marland, Jr., became the U.S. Commissioner of Education, the national right to read project was given the appropriate concern it deserved, and the entire matter of early childhood education received additional national attention. Dr. Marland helped to increase support and add momentum to the early childhood education programs of the Children's Television Workshop — "Sesame Street" and the "Electric Company."

The efforts of Secretary Richardson and Commissioner Marland to strengthen educational learning in the home gave rise to the formulation of the author's idea to compose a parents' manual for home-based, early childhood education.

This book was prepared to be used in the home by parents who might lack formal training but who desire to provide an excellent learning environment for their children. The vocabulary may seem too simplistic to some; others may find that explanations are repetitive and that, in some instances, the author is pointing out the obvious. These, however, are the inevitable consequences of attempting to give written instructions and suggestions to an audience with broadly ranging abilities and varied educational backgrounds. The deliberate purpose of the book is to provide a program of home-based, early childhood education that will reach any parent in any home. Written as a text for teaching parents in the home *how to teach their children how to learn*, the book can be used to greater extent in study groups where an interchange of parents' ideas and the sharing of their children's responses to the stimulations spelled out in the book can be discussed.

Many school systems, especially those in neighborhoods heavily populated by children of preschool age, have endorsed the policy of early childhood education and are prepared to sponsor study groups. The biblical message that the parents are the first teachers takes on a modern role — that of teaching parents to teach the child how to learn by *expanding his or her abilities to learn* from the moment he or she is born. In helping parents to cultivate these techniques by following the instructions in this book and by using educational and homemade toys, the elementary school can fill a great need in the current education scheme. For elementary schools committed to strengthening the home as a learning laboratory, toy lending libraries — together with courses of instruction for parents and correlation with such children's TV programs as "Sesame Street" and others — will constitute a rich and meaningful program of learning.

Some parents may desire to form neighborhood study groups and use this book as a reference for study and discussion sessions there. Whether it be used in a school-sponsored effort, a study group-based program in the neighborhood, or a basic reference for individual study, the book should provide a useful guideline for practicable application of the fundamental principles of early childhood education.

After parents have read the entire book and have discussed its contents either in a series of study group sessions or in individualized study, the book should be kept available for daily reference and review. An index has been prepared to help the parents readily find suggested instruction for teaching their child throughout the first five years of his or her life. Repeated study of the chapters applicable to the age of the child will also help the parent follow the program in a systematic, orderly approach to comprehensive early childhood learning.

Although parents of both boys and girls will be using this book, we have chosen to adhere to the time-established method of referring to the child in the masculine — "he, him, his." Any other reference, such as he/she, him/her, or his/hers, would make the straightforward reading of the text too complicated.

The Editors

1 Helping Your Child Build a More Powerful Intelligence

Defining and discussing the idea of intelligence are controversial and difficult. We know that some persons learn very quickly and with obvious ease, and we often refer to such persons as "very bright" or "highly intelligent." We also know that some persons are slow to learn and appear to be limited in what they can learn. It is common to refer to such persons as "slow mentally" or "mentally retarded."

To be quick of mind, to be able to grasp subtle meanings, to understand (comprehend) complex ideas (concepts) are great gifts. Educators refer to students with such abilities as "academically talented" or "intellectually superior."

Intelligence has to do with a person's *mental capacity*. It relates to the *ability to learn* as contrasted to knowledge or what has been learned. A very bright two-year-old child may have a powerful learning capacity, but he obviously has little knowledge or wisdom. A powerful intelligence shows the capacity to understand and comprehend . . . and to exercise higher mental functions. A person with a powerful intelligence has the capability of learning at a greater speed than other people and can easily grasp factors in a complex situation. This is not to imply that the most intelligent people are the most ambitious or conscientious, nor that all the desired traits or talents are embodied in a powerful intelligence. An intelligent person may be lazy, cruel, unfair, dishonest, or many

Intelligence is a person's mental capacity

other undesirable things, or he may be unhappy or unhealthy. We must seek many human traits in addition to intelligence.

Intelligence is, however, a desirable human feature embodying one of the most universal powers a person may possess. A talented musician is more capable if he has a powerful basic intellect. A person with mechanical or technical aptitudes is much more productive if he is also quick of mind. A person able to work with people is greatly aided in his efforts if he has a powerful intelligence.

Intelligence opens many doors, just as ignorance prevents progress and opportunity. No matter how bright and quick of mind one might be, he usually wishes that he could learn and understand more quickly and with greater depth. Early childhood, indeed infant development in the learning processes is therefore desirable for all children, regardless of background or ability.

Early childhood development in the learning process is desirable for all children

All parents should strive to help their children from infancy build a powerful intelligence. All children should have — as part of their heritage — the greatest opportunity to develop all their talents. Fundamental to all other abilities is the development of basic intelligence.

The Power of Parental Love

As you follow the program in this book, you will grow closer to your child. Parental love will help the child feel secure and emotionally responsive. This is the great strength of home-based, early childhood learning. Only this element — so essential to all babies and small children — can be provided in full measure by parents. A warm, intimate, and continuous loving and sharing between parent and child can grow from the parental role as the child's first teacher.

Parental love will help the child feel secure

Parents should not sacrifice the child's feelings of security and of being accepted while he is learning to respect the act of learning. Learning should be brought about naturally in an atmosphere of loving encouragement rather than through demand and pressure. Unusual achievement in terms of growth in the child's understanding is possible in a natural and relaxed home.

In the pages that follow, the techniques of teaching your child will be blended with the text content. The entire program assumes that a small child can learn as he plays and grows in the natural, loving environment of the home. The practical how-to-do-it applications at the end of each chapter, written by Mr. Arden R. Thorum, an authority on early childhood development, should substantially aid the parent to reach that goal which is desirable for the child at each succeeding age level. The result should produce a priceless gift for the child and a great sense of accomplishment for the parent.

A small child can learn while playing in the natural environment of the home

Critical Role of Parents

Not long ago, most educators believed that intelligence was almost totally fixed at birth and that quickness of mind or capacity to learn was determined by heredity. A stereotyped mental capacity of a child was universally accepted. It was believed that we should strive to teach a child all we could *within the limits of his capacity, but that we could not increase the basic capacity significantly beyond the limits inherited at the time of conception.* There have been many debates on this issue, but only in the last few years have facts on this matter become known.

We now have strong evidence that a human being can increase his intelligence. This means more than the simple fact that a normal child can learn to work twice as hard as the above-average child and make up with effort what he lacks in basic intellectual capacity. Environmental factors have much more to do with nurturing[1] intelligence than was expected even a short time ago. Presently, evidence from research gives us reason to believe that we can increase this basic intellectual power and help the normal child build his intelligence significantly beyond the usually accepted range of his intelligence quotient (IQ).

There is strong evidence that human beings can increase their learning skills

Recent research by psychologists reveals that the capacity to learn quickly and with ease can be significantly expanded beyond that inherited at birth, possibly one of the most important educational discoveries of the 20th century. This message for parents and

---

[1]For the purposes of this book, "nurturing" is used in the context of "summoning forth, protecting, feeding, and causing to grow."

WINGATE COLLEGE LIBRARY
WINGATE, N. C.

educators brings great hope and heavy responsibility for developing the intelligence of infants. Evidence that the environmental power of the home is more influential than the school places much of the responsibility on the parents.

The emphasis is placed on young children because research tells us that we must bring certain mind-nurturing experiences to children before the age of five years if we are to take advantage of this great new potential. Most of a child's basic intelligence, according to the research, *has been formed by the time he reaches school age.* Parents should keep this in mind so that the early months, when the mind is the most impressionable, are used to maximum advantage.

Basic intelligence
is formed in the
first five years
of life

Home vs the School as the Site for Early Childhood Learning

The fundamental fact that the home is where early childhood learning occurs has triggered a great debate in education circles. Some psychologists and educators advocate starting public school education at two years of age, claiming that a great opportunity will be lost if we do not start sending our two-year-olds to school where they can avail themselves of this great promise to build their intellects. Many opponents, however, do not agree. Although they recognize the potential, they argue that young children will lose much more than they will gain if we institutionalize or formalize learning this early in life. They argue that in the early months, the child needs the home and the home needs the child. They argue that schools are too large to reach the minds of tiny tots and that the home will be weakened and too much responsibility placed on the schools. Studies of home and parental influence on learning seem to support this position.

Children lose more
than they gain if
early education
is formalized

The debate also includes school finance. Some critics claim that it will take untold billions of dollars to educate two- to five-year-olds. It will also take thousands of new school buildings and vast numbers of additional teachers. Opinions of how much government and/or family should do enter this continuing debate. Many parents want the schools barred from ventures in early childhood education, while others demand an immediate response. Some critics say that it will cost more if we fail to reach the mentally retarded to give them a chance to build an intellect that helps them achieve their greatest potential. Others claim that it is unfair to reach some and not others and that early childhood education for the mentally slow places a stigma on them and deprives the normal child from building his intellect to become a superior child.

Because of the emotion, the political conflict, and the lack of public finances, it appears that public-sponsored, far-reaching, early childhood education is a long way from becoming a reality — if indeed it ever will. This places a great responsibility and challenge on the home . . . particularly upon parents who are concerned about their small children and who conscientiously desire to provide the maximum opportunities for them. Many parents eagerly accept the added burden of building the basic intellectual power in young children so that the child may be a superior student — a bright and creative human being.

The responsibility of early childhood education is on the home

The Potential of Home-Based, Early Childhood Learning with Parents as the Prime Teachers

Parents should be taught the fundamentals of early childhood education, of· how to recognize and seize upon the fleeting teaching moments in a small child's life. They should learn to teach through joyful and productive play, to apply the reinforcement theory (explained in chapter 3) in the home to create a process for learning and to stimulate the child's mind for developing cognitive powers.[2]

Parents should learn to teach through joyful and productive play

Parents should be equipped with educational toys and supplies and with simple-to-follow instructions. They should be helped to convert the child's home environment into a powerful learning laboratory so that the child will grow intellectually during those vital first five years of his life. Parents should realize that the opportunity to take full advantage of early childhood intellectual development comes only once in each child's lifetime. Most of it comes before the child enters school.

Convert the home into a learning laboratory

---

[2]"Cognitive power" is much more than merely being aware . . . it is the process of knowing in the broadest sense; that is, a child with cognitive power understands fully the concept of what is being taught so that subsequent reference to this subject will always be clear to him.

Demands on Parents' Time

As you read this book, you may become concerned about what may seem to be excessive demands upon your time to do all of the things and carry out all of the activities recommended. You will, however, find that most of the recommended activities to develop cognitive growth in your child can be carried out as you perform other routine tasks in your home. Considerable emphasis is placed upon recognizing opportune moments to teach through your daily contacts with your child while you dress him in the morning, feed or play with him during the day, take him shopping, or put him to bed at night. The techniques are casual; the teaching incidental and related to the real-life experiences of parent and child.

Recognize opportune moments to teach during the daily contacts with your child

Keep in mind that most of the recommended activities do not require additional time from busy parents, but more educationally productive use of the usual time spent by parents with their children. Also remember that each child develops differently. Do not be unduly alarmed if your child does not keep up with

Illustrations by
Nanette Nielson

the recommended activities for the age group cited in this book. Detailed instructions throughout the book will help you bring your child along at his own pace.

Educational Toys

The use of the term "educational toys" may be a mistake — for the items discussed in this book are used primarily as teaching aids and motivational tools rather than simply as playthings. However, the term has almost universal usage, and we shall continue to use it herein.

The activities discussed at the end of each chapter are designed to make use of common household items. They do not require the purchase of special toys. For those parents who wish to purchase educational toys as a supplement for household items, chapter 4 discusses the kinds of toys which are available and gives some guidelines concerning toy purchase and use.

Household items can be used as educational toys

Keep in mind that the child should have "play" toys in addition to those "learning" toys discussed in this book. The two kinds of toys serve different purposes and should be treated differently. This is also discussed in chapter 4.

Common Household Items as Teaching Aids

At the end of each chapter in this book are some practical how-to-do-it suggestions involving the use of common household items as teaching aids. These useful and easy-to-follow instructions will add to the utility and effectiveness of making concrete learning applications of the principles of learning described in the book.

Children need "hands on" experiences as they learn. They need to be able to feel, see, hear, and manipulate objects that will support and reinforce learning. The practical applications at the end of each chapter will be very useful to you in providing these concrete learning experiences for your child.

Practical Application

You can use many common household items as educational materials for teaching your child . . . macaroni, buttons, spools, cans, wrapping paper, clothes pins, a variety of containers . . . all can effectively be used to develop in your child a knowledge of basic concepts. Parents need not feel restricted if the home lacks commercial toys — since all of the same principles may be taught with household items.

The following examples show how common beans can be used by parents as a teaching device for various age groups from birth through five years of age.

Place beans in an empty can and rattle them to provide auditory stimulation for the infant.

Birth to Ten Months

Place the beans in an empty can and rattle them to provide auditory stimulation.

Ten to Eighteen Months

Place the beans in a clear plastic container which is securely sealed, and have the child watch the beans move from one end to the other.

Eighteen to Twenty-four Months

Cut out a face from homemade play dough (recipe at the end of chapter 4) and have your child use the beans to put such features as eyes, nose, mouth, etc., on the face.

Use beans to develop numerical concepts by placing four beans beside an outline of number "4."

Two to Three Years

To develop listening skills in your child, drop a few beans, one at a time, into a container and then have your child drop in the same number of beans.

Three to Four Years

Use the beans to form letters. Use them also to form numbers and to develop numerical concepts such as placing five beans on the table beside a bean outline of the number "5." You may want to

have him place them on glue or paste, but they can be successfully used without being glued down.

Four to Five Years

Space the beans so that they appear as words in a short sentence: 0 0 0 . . . 0 0 . . . 0 . . . 0 0 0. Let your child observe how you have placed them. Mix them up before letting him try it. Now have him place the beans in the same sequence.

Arrange beans to represent letters and words in a sentence. Let the child observe how you placed them. Have her place them in the same sequence.

2 General Instructions and Cautions

Most experts in the field of early childhood development are concerned that children may learn to dislike learning and even develop strong emotional blocks if overly anxious parents pressure them to levels of achievement before the children are ready. It is also feared that parents, lacking in professional training, may not recognize the limitations of very small children.

Children may learn to dislike learning if pressured by overanxious parents

Avoiding Pressure

Because of often-expressed apprehensions by educators, it is important that parents recognize the necessity of teaching the child when he is ready and when he is motivated to learn. In the use of educational toys and in the suggested games and parent-child activities that will be presented, the child must be the one to determine when he wants to participate. Be sure to avoid pressure. Be sure to observe the child carefully and take advantage of the times when he is interested and wants to participate in the learning activity. Also, be very observant to note when the child has passed the point when the learning activity is productive.

The child must determine the right teaching moment

This key concept of teaching when the child wants to learn and stopping when his interest is low must guide the parent throughout the program. The child is entitled to grow and develop happily. He must enjoy his learning activity and develop very positive attitudes toward learning. (More information on developing positive attitudes will be given in chapter 3 when the reinforcement theory is discussed.)

Peaks and Valleys in Learning

There will be high and low spots in the child's response to the learning situation

There will be periods of time in the life of almost every child when he will have a total disinterest in learning activities. There will be other times when he will be highly interested and will eagerly seek opportunities to learn and to be involved in the games and in the use of educational toys. Children go through stages of development which are related to their physical, emotional, and psychological growth. Parents should not be unduly concerned if the level of interest is irregular over a span of time. There will be high and low spots in the child's responses to the learning situation. Wise parents will adapt to these situations without conveying apprehension to the child.

Attention Span

Parents must learn to take advantage of high levels of interest and to shift to other activities when interest is low

Depending upon the nature of the learning activity, a child's attention span will vary — young children become disinterested quickly; they do not have the capability of concentrating for very long. When using educational toys and parent-child games, parents must be carefully observant of the learning situation. They must learn to take advantage of high levels of interest and to shift to other learning activities or postpone the learning activity entirely when the child's attention span is low. Children become restless at certain periods of the day. By observing closely, the parent will learn to distinguish the child's interest level in any particular situation. From that knowledge, the parent should be able to determine when the optimum learning situation has passed. The best learning opportunity for the child will have expired when he is no longer paying attention . . . when he becomes irritable or fidgety or when he starts asking questions not related to the learning situation. At this point the learning activity should be changed, or the entire period for participation in the program should be postponed.

Being observant and understanding of the varied attention capabilities and being able to transfer that knowledge into a shift in activity or a change of pace are very critical skills for a parent to develop. As you work with your child, be conscious of the need to be sensitive to his attention span.

Learning to Enjoy the Teaching-Learning Situation

Parents should engage a child in developmental experiences only when it can be a joyful activity for both parents and child. It is important to recognize that when parents are under stress, it is unwise for them to enter into teaching activities with their children. Most parents know when they feel up to the challenge.

Timing is extremely important in the development of very young children; emotional circumstances are crucial. Both parent and child must be prepared for a joyful experience together. They must be relaxed, with tension at a minimum level. Parents should recognize this and think about it often. They should review the learning experience after it has occurred and ask themselves if the experience has been pleasant for the child. They should also ask themselves if the atmosphere was relaxed and if there was ample opportunity for pleasant interaction, for laughing and happy responses.

Both parent and child must be ready for a joyful experience together

The early childhood development program in the home should not in any way follow patterns at school. Preschool children are far too young to have a structured, regular program of instruction patterned after school curricula. The parents should therefore not think of themselves as teachers in the formal sense. The entire environment must be natural and spontaneous so that each learning experience developed by the parent will carry out the sequential learning activities contained in this program and at the same time permit the child to set the pace.

The home-based teaching program should not follow the structured curriculum of the school

During the teaching and learning experiences, the parent should play a different "role" from that played during the rest of the day, relating to the child in a mode of relaxed play and conversation. The parent must let each of the child's responses flow naturally from the previous response. Parents must recognize when to have a great variety of activities and when to seize upon a high-interest point to get a basic concept or a particularly difficult skill across to the child.

Establishing the Optimum Physical Environment

It is important for the parent to think constantly about the physical surroundings and to establish the optimum environment for enhancing the learning situation. This should vary from one situation to another, depending upon the type of learning activity.

Distractions should be kept to a minimum

Distractions should be kept to a minimum. Parents should seek ways of developing the physical surroundings so that they will contribute to the learning situation. A pleasant environment, conducive to learning, should be planned.

Many homes are not sufficiently "child centered," and many children must make too many adaptations and adjustments to the adult mode of living. Bright colors, cheerful pictures and paintings, and child-oriented furnishings will add to the total opportunity to give the child the finest environmental situation during this critical first five years of life. Parents

The home must be a bright and cheerful setting for preschool learning

should remember that once these opportune days, weeks, and months have passed, they cannot relive them with the child. They should remember that research tells us that a child gains the greatest portion of his intelligence during those first five years of his life. In this sense, the home is the first classroom and the parent the first teacher.

We urge parents to look at their homes and determine if they are child centered. The priceless years of early childhood will be gone all too soon. Make your homes truly conducive to the maximum environmental circumstances that will nurture the growth of your child to the greatest extent possible. More specific information on the home as a learning laboratory for the child will be presented in chapter 3.

Practical Application

In a sense, almost all experiences can become learning experiences if a little extra effort is offered. The home, which is the child's world, can also become his learning laboratory. Parents should examine the surroundings of the home and use them to explain different concepts to the child. Be aware of differences in space and size, temperatures, textures, and various patterns and forms. Take advantage of situations to further your child's cognitive progression.

One small example illustrates the principle of cause and effect at the breakfast table while you are preparing your child's cereal:

1. Place the dry cereal in front of your child and have him taste it. Call his attention to how dry and crunchy it feels.

2. Add milk, and let him examine the changes that take place. (The cereal starts to absorb the milk and turn soft.)

3. Draw his attention to the taste of the cereal before and after sugar is added.

4. Find out if he understands the principles involved by asking him:

> "What would happen if I put sugar on your toast?"
>
> "What would happen if I put milk on your toast?"
>
> "Why does your cereal taste different when I put sugar on it?"

Although this experience might occur at the three- to four-year age level, similar learning activities should be built into daily routines at all ages. The concept of size relationships can also be taught at this and earlier ages by showing your child various-sized potatoes to demonstrate large, larger, largest. Tactile abilities can

Show the child how crunchy dry cereal is to taste.

Add milk and let him see the changes that occur.

Have him taste it before and after sugar is added.

The concept of size relationship can be taught by comparing similar objects for variations in size.

be enhanced by placing an object in a bag without your child's seeing it ahead of time, and then having him identify what it is by relying on his sense of touch. Sound identification can be practiced by calling the child's attention to sounds heard around the home and by asking him to identify them.

Place an object in a bag so the child can identify the object by relying on her sense of touch only.

3 Learning to Think and Act from the Child's Viewpoint

Many forces enter into the rearing of a child in the home. During the first five years, childhood experiences will fortify the child with the capabilities to obtain and retain knowledge throughout his life. The "knowledge" experiences are discussed below.

Empathy

Empathy is the imaginative projection of oneself into the being or circumstance of another. Parents should, in the time that they spend teaching the child, try to empathize. Through close observation and practice in watching the response of the child, the ability to empathize can be developed. As you work and play with your child, study his reactions and learn everything you can about him. Strive to understand why he does what he does. The more you know, the more effective you will be as a parent and teacher.

As you work and play with your child, study the reactions . . . try to empathize

Reinforcement as a Basic Principle in Teaching

There is likely no other principle of teaching and learning that is more important to the child and to the parent than the reinforcement theory — an awareness that most of the experiences must be successful and reinforcing to the child. Rebellion and dislike for learning will be the result if this paramount principle is ignored.

It is important that parents learn about the principle of reinforcement and how they can use it in

Rebellion and dislike for learning result from lack of reinforcement

helping the child develop a more powerful intelligence. If parents understand this principle and observe how reinforcement can lead a child to desirable or undesirable behavior, they will be more conscious of many actions that unwittingly work against the purposes and outcomes they are seeking. Most human beings persist in doing those things that are rewarding and pleasurable. If, for example, a child cries when he is refused candy and if the parent responds by "giving in," the parent is obviously encouraging an undesirable habit.

Parents should use reinforcement to the child's advantage

A small baby soon learns that crying gets attention — his way of communicating that he is uncomfortable or wants something. While it would be absurd to recommend that parents ignore crying, it is important that the parent be aware of responses made to crying so that the parent is not unconsciously reinforcing behavior that must be changed or eliminated later in the child's life. Some of this cannot be avoided for it is part of rearing a tiny infant. The point is that the parent should be conscious of this reinforcing behavior and use it to the child's advantage. Not only do you teach by your *actions*, you also teach by your *reactions*.

The child should be praised and encouraged along with being corrected

The positive use of reinforcement calls for rewarding the desirable response and keeping to a minimum (or eliminating where possible) the rewards for undesirable behavior. A reinforcement-conscious parent will be very careful about using negative responses and saying "no" too often. Instead, positive and rewarding responses can be used to lead the child in an affirmative way (rather than negative responses that will drive the child through punishment).

Children have a better self-image if they learn through rewards instead of through punishment

The parent should be particularly conscious in the teaching and learning experiences suggested in this book to use the reinforcement theory. Plainly stated, children will have a better self-image if they learn through rewards rather than through punishment. Parents should be careful about saying "No, that is wrong" in an unpleasant voice. This does not mean that children should learn only about their correct responses. Obviously, it is necessary for a child to know when his response is incorrect. The method of communication, however, should convey information that the response is incorrect in a manner that will minimize negativeness and will lead rather than drive the child.

If, for example, the child misses a key step in a learning game, the parent should emphasize some of the child's previous correct answers at the same time that he learns that he just missed the key question. He should be praised and encouraged at the same time that he is corrected for error. Parents get in the "no" and "don't" habit of communicating with children. This is sadly demonstrated by studies of vocabulary development in young children which indicate that the word *no* is one of the first words spoken by most children.

Parents, in their anxiety to help the child, correct too much and lead and reinforce too little. Strive to use positive words most of the time in your communication with your child. Use the words "no" and "don't" sparingly. If parents are careful in their manner of correction, learning will be a happy experience, and the child will seek more opportunities to be involved in it.

Adjusting the Level of Difficulty

The parent must be very conscious of the "level of difficulty" at which the child is working. Experts on learning tell us that the level of difficulty for a child should be adjusted so that he is making correct responses approximately eight out of every ten times he is asked to respond in a learning situation. This keeps the entire experience "reinforcing" in its outcome and minimizes the number of times that the child has to be corrected and told, even in a positive way, that his response to the learning situation was incorrect.

The level of difficulty should be adjusted until the child can respond correctly about eight out of ten times

Observing the child's response, the parent should make the question easier or the learning game less difficult if the child is not responding correctly in approximately eight out of ten questions. When educational toys are used, a less difficult or more challenging game can usually be selected to meet the performance level of the child. In the less formal situation — where the parent is questioning and the child is responding — the solution is to ask less challenging or more difficult questions. As the parent and child work together, it will become increasingly easy for the parent to adjust the level of difficulty to meet the child's needs.

Success is contagious. In our eagerness to get the child to move ahead rapidly, or in our concern that he may be behind, it is very easy to push too hard or to move the child to a level of difficulty where his responses are most often incorrect. This is self-defeating and must be avoided at all costs.

There must be sufficient challenge to cause the child to feel accomplishment

The parent should realize that there must be sufficient challenge in the learning situation so that the child is learning, advancing, and attaining a feeling of accomplishment. If the situation is so easy that the child is responding correctly 100 percent of the time, he has already learned the task, and the level of difficulty must be advanced. Parents should remember that the 80 percent correct response principle is desirable. It may not be necessary to measure this precisely in the informal use of educational toys, learning games, and other teaching and learning activities. It is important, however, to be conscious of the fact that most of the responses must be correct and that the child must be on a level of difficulty where the parent can genuinely praise him often and reward him for his correct responses. Many times throughout the teaching and learning activities of our program, we will urge the parent to be conscious of the use of the power of reinforcement in the teaching situation. This chapter (and particularly this section of the chapter) may need to be reviewed often by the parent in order for the principles of reinforcement to become a natural part of the parents' teaching behavior.

Make your awareness of reinforcement a guide to your teaching behavior

Be sure that you understand the principle of reinforcement. *Make your awareness of the power of reinforcement a guide to your teaching behavior.* The application of this principle may be the most important teaching technique you will ever learn. Your behavior will largely determine the attitude and success of your child in his early childhood education.

Parents should consider the following examples in thinking through how the reinforcement principle can be used in the home to obtain the desired results:

Example A mother decides that her two-year-old is ready for toilet training. She begins by casually placing the child on the toilet at intervals when she suspects that he is ready for bladder or bowel elimination.

Comment The first experience should be a pleasant one. The mother should carefully select the proper time when the child is not sleepy or irritable. Pleasant and optimistic voice tones should be used. Simple and positive explanations should be made. The experience should be very brief. If the act is not successful, the parent should express mild encouragement and approval anyway. If it is successful, the parent should praise the child and encourage him to let the mother know when the physical need is felt for elimination.

Make the first experience in any situation a pleasant one

Example A 3½-year-old child keeps begging to eat between meals. The parent has determined that the child's nutrition is adequate and that he should not be hungry an hour or two after he has eaten. The child is persistent and increases the pressure until the parent gives in "just to keep him quiet."

Comment This is applying reinforcement to develop undesired behavior and bad eating habits. The child learns from the success of pressure and persistence that the parent will eventually give in to his demands. The behavior of whining and the habit of eating between meals are unwittingly taught by the parent through misapplication of the reinforcement theory.

Apply the rein-forcement principle in desirable, not undesirable, circumstances

Example A parent desires to develop number discrimination skills through use of an educational toy that builds this capacity. When the atmosphere is relaxed and it is play-time for the child, the parent asks for and receives a positive request to the suggestion that the parent and child play the number discrimination game. The two start playing, and the child responds correctly to only half of the items. The parent, knowing that a successful experience is essential to the child's future attitude, immediately moves the level of difficulty back to where the child had been answering about eight out of every ten problems correctly. This gives the child a feeling of accomplishment, but the level of difficulty is still challenging, as evidenced by the few incorrect responses that are made from time to time. After some time, the child begins to show disinterest. Although the parent is anxious for the child to continue, the game is stopped without pressure or unpleasantness when the attention of the child starts to decline. The child is praised for his success as the game ends, despite the fact that the parent would have been pleased with more progress.

Comment This wise parent knows that success is measured by how much desire the child has in continuing the game. This cannot be done if the child experiences failure too many times. Thus the level of difficulty was adjusted so that most of the child's attempts were successful. The child ended the game too soon to please the parent, but the parent did not pressure the child when gentle persuasion did not succeed in getting agreement to continue. The child learned the results of each learning attempt and knew, when incorrect responses were made, what the correct response should have been.

Always adjust the level of difficulty so that your child feels success rather than failure

This represents the application of the reinforcement principle in a direct teaching and learning situation involving the use of creative play.

Talking to Your Child

A child can learn much from conversation; moreover, conversation and the resultant vocabulary development during the early years of a child's life will help to build his cognitive power. In conversation, of course, words are symbols consisting of sounds created by the vocal cords. For a child who does not yet have a vocabulary and who has not mastered the capacity to get meanings from sounds made by the vocal cords, this is indeed a complex and challenging learning situation. Parents should remember what was emphasized about empathy earlier in this chapter. You must know that listening and getting meaning from sounds require ability to associate these sounds with something familiar to the child. This is more complicated than one might think, particularly if this task is analyzed from the point of view of the child. Remember that the child is beginning with zero vocabulary.

Very young children need constant spoken vocabulary stimulation, and parents should converse frequently with them. Some studies of child behavior indicate that children will make earlier attempts at speaking and will jabber and make conversational mimicry if, during the early months of their lifetime, they live in an environment where they are talked to frequently. Even at an early age when a parent may not think a child is understanding, it is important that conversation (even if it is a one-way discussion) occur frequently. Exposure to language and vocabulary building is very important. The entire five-year period is one of building vocabulary and developing language skills.

Children learn to recognize words before they learn to speak

As will be discussed in subsequent instructions and suggestions in this text, children should begin to develop a listening or "word recognition" vocabulary before they can speak. Using carefully spoken words — such as "shoes" when the young baby's shoes are being put on and "fingers" when you touch or he uses his fingers — will help to build an identification and listening vocabulary before the child actually learns to speak. Repetition of plainly spoken, short words is very important. The proper words used when the child is initially exposed will help to simplify the child's being able to understand.

The word "dog" is much less confusing to a child than to teach him that a dog is a "doggie" and then later to tell him that "doggie" and "dog" are the same thing. This principle also applies to "train" and "choo choo twain." Often, parents think they are speaking on the child's level when they use childlike words. This only adds to the learning burden of the child. Parents can use the proper words and speak them with enthusiasm in a tone that creates response from the child without resorting to copying words they

Parents should teach the proper pronunciation of words, not baby talk have heard other young children use when first learning to speak.

Parents will also help children build vocabularies if two or more words that denote the same thing can be avoided; for example, if a mother calls a cat a "kitten" and a "kitty" as well as a "cat," she can cause confusion for a young child struggling to master complex sound symbols that identify an unfamiliar world filled with unfamiliar objects and things. Please be sure to thoughtfully avoid confusion in this regard.

Words such as "too," "to," and "two" are often used freely in the same sentence ("It's *too* late *to* play with your *two* cars"). Proper words, clear pronunciation, and an avoidance of confusing terms (*"No,* I don't *know"* or *"Close* the door and hang up your *clothes"*) will do much to help the child.

Teach the difficult concepts, such as right and left hand, carefully

In teaching right- and left-side and right- and left-hand concepts, a thoughtless teacher may say to a small child "right," meaning that he is correct when he points to his left hand. Parents must be exceedingly conscious of words used in conversation with very young children.

If a child is to develop a keen intellect and a powerful means of expressing thoughts, he should be exposed to a rich vocabulary. Repeating the names of objects which continually surround the child will help build vocabulary power. Detailed emphasis will be given in building a more powerful intelligence through the use of language in subsequent chapters of this book. Emphasis is given at this time so that parents will know from the outset that conversation and vocabulary building are extremely important and should be properly developed from the very first months of life and continued throughout the remainder of the entire program of home-based, early childhood instruction.

The Home as a Learning Laboratory

The home must provide exposure to books, pictures, colors, and shapes

To be successful in building the child's intellectual power, the home must provide continuous exposure to a wide variety of experiences. These experiences should stimulate the mind of the child and expose him to circumstances where the limits of his mind will be stretched. In any home where children are growing up, the most important function is to nurture development and bring to fruition all of the latent talents of the child.

Exposure to books, to illustrations and pictures, to puzzles, to stimulating colors and shapes, and to a rich array of sounds, smells, tastes, and touching and listening opportunities should be planned. Variety and change of environmental stimulation are very important. Parents should constantly be thinking of how to add depth and breadth to the experiences which are provided in the home. Learning takes place when affirmative action is required from the learner. The teaching methods described in this manual and in related supporting materials will call for an active response from the learner.

Learning takes place when affirmative action is required from the listener

Many television programs may be useful in this regard. Parents should supplement the course of instruction provided in this book with related toys and materials from toy lending libraries and with regular exposure to children's TV programs. Viewing and listening to such programs will fall short of a total early childhood development program; however, they will be a useful enrichment and an added environmental dimension that should be used by parents. Because TV viewing is a somewhat passive activity for the young, it should therefore be considered as having only that enrichment value which can be greatly enhanced through active follow-up by the parent. The essential elements of the many children's programs, such as "Sesame Street," will be incorporated into the contents of this book. Therefore, these TV shows developed for the very young should be used but not relied upon as anything even closely approaching a maximum effort at early childhood education.

Television viewing should be enhanced through active follow-up by the parents to teach the precepts shown

Parents should be conscious of the home as a learning laboratory for the child. A variety of materials that will keep the child constantly exposed to learning circumstances should be provided. Recorded music and stimulating, colorfully illustrated books can serve as added supplementary and enrichment materials in a home consciously prepared to perform the function of providing maximum intellectual stimulation for the child. Parents should look at the home from the child's perspective and should often think of the home as a stimulating learning environment which will lend

Parents should look at the home as a learning environment for their child

maximum support to parental efforts to nurture the full potential for helping the child build a superior mind.

The Child's Self-Image

It is important that the child grow up with a positive self-image. This comes from successful experience and from a sense of progress and accomplishment each day. Parents should relate to the child in such a way as to provide a feeling of belonging and a feeling of worthiness, which requires a great amount of loving and listening by the parents.

The child must develop a positive self-image from day-to-day accomplishments

The listening part of this self-image building effort should be taken seriously. Parents should seek to have the child express himself. They should, through listening and encouraging expression, seek to know what the child is thinking. They should try to encourage the child to express any fears and apprehensions that he might have. This will yield valuable information to the parents as well as provide a useful outlet for the child's feelings. These listening sessions should help the parents get feedback on their teachings as well as indicate the child's responses to these stimuli. Perceptive parents will learn how to adjust and adapt teaching strategies from what they learn during these listening sessions.

Parents should encourage their child to express doubts and fears to them

The child should be helped to develop a positive "can do" attitude toward learning and toward himself as an individual capable of doing a number of useful things. Keeping the level of difficulty adjusted to the child's needs will help in building a good self-image. (Review the material on reinforcement in the first part of this chapter if you need to refresh your memory on adjusting the level of difficulty to meet the child's learning needs.)

The child should develop a positive "can do" attitude

Practical Application

Parents should familiarize themselves with the teaching principles explained in this book and should apply them when engaging in the recommended activities. Remember to keep the following key points in mind:

1. Develop an empathy for your child . . . try to visualize this mammoth world from his point of view. This will come naturally, to some extent, as you observe him acquiring a new skill, but learn to appreciate the awesomeness of life and be patient with him as you guide him to learn more about his environment.

Develop an empathy for your child. Do your best to visualize the world from his point of view.

2. Adjust your own emotions so that you feel free to take the time to be with your child. Remember that these teaching moments can be brief and still be very effective, but you must put other thoughts aside so that you can concentrate upon the activity and your child's responses to it.

3. Do not feel that, once begun, each task has to be completed. If the child is not motivated at the particular time you wish to teach, or if he appears to be losing interest, stop your teaching activities for the time being. It is more important to engage in the teaching-learning experience when the child is attentive, not when he appears to be under pressure to complete a task simply because it was started.

4. Be aware of your child's visual and physical limitations; that is, place the objects where he can easily see and reach them, and be sure that they fit his age group for manipulating them. Make the necessary adjustments so that your face and his are approximately at the same level.

5. Plan ahead to have the required materials available to avoid any interruptions during the activity.

6. Examine all the items you will use to make certain that they are safe, that they perform their function (are not broken), and that they are easy for the child to manipulate.

These teaching moments can be brief and still be effective, but you must put other thoughts aside.

Make the necessary adjustments so that your face and the child's face are at about the same level.

Develop your own activities to provide learning experiences, but don't make them too difficult.

Take advantage of all that nature has to teach in the out-of-doors. Call attention to fine details.

7. Orient your home to include some conveniences for your child. Have a footstool for him to stand on while he is washing his hands; lower the clothes bar in his closet so that his clothing is easy for him to reach; put his personal belongings (such as his toothbrush) within easy reach.

8. Develop your own individualized activities for the child's learning experiences similar to those presented at the end of each chapter. Make sure that they are not too difficult, but will provide positive reinforcement and will promote the preliminary skills essential to acquiring more advanced skills as your child grows.

9. Do not become discouraged if it appears that your child has lost a skill you thought he had learned. As explained in the text, there are peaks and valleys in learning in which children go through different developmental stages. Especially, do not express disappointment to the child. He needs all the *positive* reinforcement you can give him.

10. Take advantage of all that nature has to teach in the out-of-doors. Expose your child not only to the vastness of his surroundings, but call his attention to fine details, such as an ant crawling up a tree or snow melting and dripping.

Orient your home to include some **conveniences** for the child; lower the clothes bar in his closet.

4 Household Items and Educational Toys as Teaching Aids

Toys that have educational value — blocks with letters or numbers on them, balls or other geometric shapes of different sizes and colors, etc. — can be appropriately useful in teaching children. In addition, there are always in the home many items that can be successfully used as teaching aids. These kinds of toys and the libraries that contain the manufactured variety are discussed in this chapter.

Educational toys are useful in teaching children

Toy Lending Libraries

During the past few years, a number of schools have initiated a program of lending educational toys to parents of preschool children. This movement has been greatly accelerated by the research and development efforts of the Far West Laboratory for Educational Research and Development of Berkeley, California. Within a brief time, toy lending libraries will, the author believes, become almost universally available in elementary schools across the nation.

In subsequent chapters of this book, reference will be made to toy lending libraries or educational toy libraries. Where toys are available on loan from schools, parents are urged to use them as extensively as possible. It is very likely that such lending programs will not be available to large numbers of parents. It is suggested that parents obtain access to educational toys either through direct purchase or through cooperative purchase by a neighborhood study group. However, if the cost of a set of educational toys is

Parents should use educational toys — either homemade, borrowed from a toy library, or purchased

beyond the budget of the parent or neighborhood group and if toys are not available from a neighborhood school, parents should substitute common household objects where possible. One advantage of using the toy library is the fact that each toy is accompanied by simple instructions for its specific use. Although the toy library is very useful and will help to motivate children to learn through play, much can be accomplished through use of items around the home.

Parents should not feel that their program of home-based, early childhood teaching will be a failure if an educational toy library is not available. Through some creative use of items commonly found around the home (see suggestions at the end of each chapter), parents and children will find many opportunities to play and learn together in the program of instruction described in this book.

Educational Toys That Stimulate Learning

In the following paragraphs, we shall discuss the kinds of toys that are applicable to different age levels and those that encompass visual, audio, and tactile (touch) sensations for the child. This discussion will serve as a general introduction . . . more specific instruction will be found in the chapters that follow.

Crib Toys

Toys for the very young infant (prescribed for teaching strategies in chapter 5) have been designed to stimulate the sensory experiences of the infant during the age of four months to the time when he is able to creep (crawl). Such toys should be colorful so that they attract the child's vision as soon as he is able to see and focus his eyes. They should, if possible, stimulate the child to want to reach (exercise), thus providing practice in coordinating his arm and leg muscles. Some crib toys should be audible to stimulate the sense of hearing; they should be responsive to hands and feet that come into contact with them. They should excite and stimulate curiosity.

Crib toys should be colorful as well as audible to stimulate visual and listening capabilities

Parents of infants should have a variety of crib toys available. The toys should be changed frequently so that they are not commonplace to the sight, touch, and hearing. Their use is to make the crib a more responsive and stimulative environment. Variety of

Crib toys should be changed often for variety

color, shape, sound, and functional response must be provided.

Most educational toy libraries begin with toys and accompanying instructions for children from 18 months on. Since crib toys may be purchased in most department stores, they are usually not included in toy libraries; however, Olympus Publishing Company has developed a set of toys that start at birth. Parents should shop around in various stores and be alert for opportunities to select a variety of crib toys. The more sound, color, and touch stimulation for the child, the greater will be his growth opportunity during the time that he is a crib-bound infant.

Toys for the Creeper

By the time the child has attained the physical capacity to creep, he has also gained the ability to reach, grasp, listen, focus his eyes, imitate, and respond to various kinds of stimulation. Homemade and educational toys (prescribed for activities recommended in chapters 5 and 6) should stimulate the curiosity of the child and sharpen his perception. Toys that will help the child develop listening skills should be provided. Toys that require the child to see differences in shapes and colors are also useful.

For the creeper, toys should stimulate curiosity and sharpen perception

The child needs muscle activity and experiences in learning coordination of his hands and feet with his vision. Toys that stimulate use of his larger muscles and those that require his hands to reach and grasp in coordination with his sight should be used.

Toys That Teach Colors, Numbers, and the Alphabet

Most toy libraries provide games that teach color identification, numbers and number concepts, and the letters of the alphabet (prescribed for activities recommended in chapters 7, 8, 9, and 11). Effective toys are designed to make truly creative play from efforts to master these concepts. Toy libraries with accompanying instructions usually describe several games on different levels of difficulty. These games provide variety and new challenges for the child. Parents will also find opportunities to create additional games from the toys contained in most of the toy libraries. Most parents, as they observe their children using educational toys, will think of other games that can be

Educational toys can aid in teaching colors, numbers, and letters

created by the parent to provide more learning opportunities for the child.

Toys that create a joyful and attention-holding response are usually effective in teaching. The learning comes without awareness of effort since the concentration is on the game. This is, of course, the great value of educational toys and toy libraries.

Toys That Teach Sight, Sound, and Touch Discrimination

The preschool child should enter formal schooling with his senses developed and his ability to use them to provide information to his thinking processes sharpened as keenly as possible. He must be able to listen to sounds that are nearly the same and detect the differences. He must be able to look at objects and pictures that are almost identical and be able to see slight differences. He must be able to identify objects that he cannot see by touching and feeling them to form mental images of them.

Parents should use toys that teach sight, sound, and touch discrimination

Most toy libraries have toys that help to sharpen the use of these senses (prescribed for activities recommended in chapters 7 through 11). The games are easily played and the directions usually brief and easy to understand and follow. Parents should use these toys designed to develop keen use of the senses of sight, touch, and hearing. The results may not become apparent until the child faces reading and arithmetic instruction in the formal school situation, but the parents should not neglect the developmental opportunities provided by these toys.

Educational Toys and Goals

Your child must reach two goals that may seem to conflict with each other: He must develop his latent mental powers to the maximum extent possible, and he must learn to enjoy learning and to develop wholesome attitudes toward his educational experiences.

Children not only must develop mental powers, but also enjoyment of learning

Educational toys should help parents reach these somewhat contradictory purposes. These toys are challenging because they do more than entertain — most educational toys require the use of two or more of the senses and involve physical as well as mental activity. Since most toys require two persons to play the games, the additional advantage of involving the parent is provided.

Importance of Following Instructions

The directions accompanying the toys from the libraries emphasize the necessity for the parent to permit the child to determine when he is ready to play a game and when he wants to stop. Parents should heed this advice. It is advisable to begin when the child is eager and to stop when his response is high so that the child will look forward to additional experiences with the toys.

Many parents, in their eagerness to see the child make progress, may pressure or attempt to coax the child to play. Research with educational toys has proved this to be a serious mistake in the strategy of teaching. The premise of this entire book is based upon play as a means of learning. The games must be child centered and child directed.

A wise parent will study the child and respond to his signals while he is using educational toys. Through extra effort by the parent, playtime that turns into incidental learning experiences will pay the rich dividends intended by the designers of educational toys. Even the best toys from these lending libraries will be ineffective if not properly used by the parent. Educational toys should not become commonplace to the child. Unlike ordinary toys, these from the toy libraries have a specific purpose. Be sure to put them away when they are not in use. Let the child have his regular toys available at any time. Make the educational toys *special* and the occasion when they are used to be anticipated and appreciated.

Let the child's interest in the game determine the time to teach

Educational toys should not become commonplace to the child

Use educational toys only during the teaching time

Toys as a Means of Developing Abstract Reasoning Powers

For the children in the fourth year of life, experiences with educational toys (used in activities recommended in chapters 12 and 13) should lead to development of ability to reason and derive judgments after weighing multiple factors in a game situation. Be sure to use the toys in your library to provide a mind-stretching interplay of the more complex games when your child has reached the age of four.

Application of the number concepts and use of simple arithmetic skills may be provided through most toy libraries. The use of toys in addition and subtraction games will make fun out of practice and drill

Games that apply number and color skills develop cognitive power

if skillfully executed by the parents. Games that apply arithmetic skill with color identification and with use of geometric shapes will provide unusually rich opportunity for development of cognitive power. Children who master these capacities to use a combination of three or more skills in a fairly complex game will be reaching levels of ability that will lead them to become very capable and intellectually powerful students when they attain school age.

Most toy libraries do not provide checkers and chess games that are recommended in chapter 14. These games are somewhat commonplace and can be obtained without much expense. They are, however, extremely effective as cognitive power builders. Parents should provide children (who display the capability) with opportunities to play these games as often as interest demands. Needless to say, not all children of preschool age will have developed the ability to skillfully play checkers and chess.

Try to play games as often as your child's interest demands

Characteristics of a Good Toy Library

Criteria of a good toy lending library

An effective educational toy lending library should meet the following criteria:

(1) Provide a broad range of experiences requiring abilities ranging from simple skills to progressively complex and difficult performance

(2) Provide learning experiences in: (a) colors, (b) numbers, (c) geometric shapes, (d) alphabet recognition, (e) arithmetic skill building, (f) listening and hearing discrimination skills, (g) tactile skills, (h) visual discrimination skills, (i) organization, classification, and sorting skills

(3) Be easily assembled and easily used by parents and children without requiring excessive time in preparation for the educational games

(4) Have simple-to-follow instructions that do not require extensive study and review before use

(5) Be rugged in construction and durable enough to withstand heavy use and some abuse from active children

(6) Be easily stored in the home so that they can be taken out and put away without difficulty

(7) Be reasonably economical so that parents do not have to make a large investment to acquire them

(8) Be packaged separately so that school and cooperative neighborhood toy libraries may check out one toy or group of toys without destroying the value or utility of other toys in the library

(9) Be free from hazards that may injure children (no sharp edges, but constructed of materials that will be perfectly safe in the hands of infants)

(10) Provide a device that will teach the child parts of the body (such as nose, ears, legs, hair, etc.)

Function of Educational Toys

Educational toys differ from ordinary toys in that they are designed to teach certain concepts and build specific skills. They are designed to use the child's natural desire to play and to have new experiences. Most educational toys have been tested with children in actual learning-playing circumstances. Results have been evaluated and written instructions developed to eliminate ambiguity and emphasize clarity of understanding. Since the attention span of small children is short, many educational toy games have a number of variations that add to the versatility of use.

Toy libraries are designed to use a child's natural desire to play

Small children have very active, absorbent minds. When the instinct to play and the capacity to learn are linked together, the results are extremely rewarding. Educational toy libraries have been designed to use the child's drive to know and his yearning to play and interact with others.

Link the child's instinct to play with his capacity to learn

Availability of Various Educational Toys and Toy Libraries

A number of respected firms have developed valuable educational toys. Most manufacturers, however, market toys separately and not as a complete library designed to support a total program of early childhood education. The major problem with educational toy programs of most large, nationwide department store chains is that a system of instruction has not been designed to help parents move progressively with the child through the first five years of his life.

The Far West Laboratory for Educational Research and Development has developed a library of toys (for children three to five years of age) that has been tested in a number of schools in the western United States. These toys (sold by General Learning Corporation) have been extensively tested, and evaluation results indicate that they can be used with confidence.

Olympus Publishing Company recently developed an educational toy library (for children from birth to five years of age) that teaches many of the same concepts as those emphasized in the Far West Laboratory toy program. The toys have also been tested with groups of children by mothers of preschool children. Several revisions and improvements in the toys and accompanying written instructions have made the toys effective as teaching aids. A unique feature of the Olympus Publishing Company toys is that they are packaged in small bags, and the entire library is packaged in one large duffel bag. This makes storage, access, and lending functions more easily accomplished.

Educational toys with written instructions have been developed for home use

Although there may be other complete educational toy libraries, the author examined and evaluated only the Far West and Olympus toys. Both toy libraries will effectively support the instructions recommended in this book.

Practical Application

Although there are many excellent educational toys on the market, one primary goal of the recommended activities in this book is to use as educational toys materials found in the home.

Play dough and finger paint from the following recipes need not be made at this time. They are placed in this chapter for your convenience. When instructions for their use appear in subsequent chapters, refer to the recipes here.

Play Dough

1½ cups flour
½ cup salt
½ cup water
¼ teaspoon liquid (dishwashing) soap
Several drops of food coloring

Mix the flour and salt together. Add water, food coloring, and soap and mix well. If dough appears too dry, add more water; if too wet, add more flour until it is of a consistency to be rolled on a floured board. When not in use, store in an airtight container in a cool place.

Finger Paint

2 cups flour
2 teaspoons salt
½ cup water
Several different food colorings

Beat the above ingredients (except food coloring) until mixture is smooth. Add two cups of hot water and boil mixture until it is clear. Divide into as many portions (in small bowls) as you desire for different colors. Add food colorings of different hues, one color to a bowl, and stir each bowlful with a separate spoon. (You can create additional colors by using red and blue to make purple, red and yellow to make orange, and blue and yellow to make green.

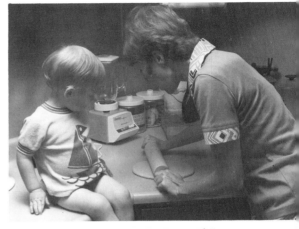

Play dough should be mixed to a consistency that it can be rolled flat on a floured board.

Homemade finger paint can be mixed from flour, salt, water, and several assorted food colorings.

Let the child watch the process of making finger paint, and have him assist whenever possible.

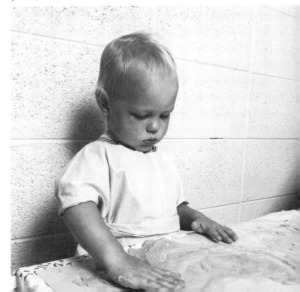

An empty shoe box makes an appealing pull toy. It can be left plain or decorated as you desire.

Wide-mouthed plastic containers can be used to teach many different concepts, such as pouring.

Containers are helpful teaching aids in the bath, in the sandpile, and at many other learning times.

Let your child watch this process, and point out to him how the two colors blend to make a new color.) Store at room temperature in tightly covered containers such as plastic margarine tubs. (You can also make finger paint from instant pudding mixes by adding enough liquid to make the desired consistency.)

Your child will also get hours of entertainment from easily constructed toys such as the following:

Pull Toy

A shoe box
An empty spool
A piece of string at least two
    feet long
A popsicle stick

In one end of the shoe box, punch a hole large enough for the string to fit through it. Thread the string through the hole, and tie the popsicle stick to the string inside the box. Pull the stick snugly against the box (you may want to tape it in place). Tie the empty spool to the other end of the string by threading the string through the hole in the spool and looping it back over the spool so that it can be tied around itself. (This will make a convenient "handle" for your child to grasp.) The box can be decorated with leftover birthday or Christmas wrapping paper, with crayon drawings, or just left plain. Let your child help you with the decorating.

Sand Buckets

Plastic containers
Spoons or plastic or metal
    cups

Equip your child with wide-mouthed, plastic containers (use clean mop buckets; plastic milk bottles with the tops trimmed and smoothed; or full-bottomed, plastic mixing bowls) that he can use outdoors as sand buckets or indoors to hold such items as empty spools, clothes pins, etc. These containers can be used later on to sort colors or to add and subtract amounts (see chapters 8 and 10) when you are teaching your child the concept of colors and numbers.

Float these "sand buckets" in his bathtub where you can use them to teach many other concepts . . . pouring, sinking (cause and effect concept), learning quantity (more or less water in the container), and engaging in water play activities.

Begin to orient yourself to the educational uses of household items and you will discover the excitement of creating new toys from your own ideas and materials.

Use household items to teach such concepts as the sorting of colors or adding and subtracting amounts.

Orient yourself to the educational uses of household items; create toys from your own materials.

5 Learning during the First Ten Months of Life

With the background information provided in the first four chapters of this book, we are now ready for instruction and intensive discussion about what, how, and when to teach. The first two chapters are important for parents as a theoretical foundation and as basic guideline material to be used throughout the entire course of instruction and the full period of the parental responsibility to the child as his first and most important teacher.

Remember that a child's feelings have a profound impact on learning. The factors we cannot teach you as a parent are the specific feelings and emotional responses of your child. We can emphasize problems and generalize from what has been learned about most children and from how most children respond, but each child is an entirely different human being. Parents realize this more than anyone else. We emphasize again that the parent should watch the emotional and attitudinal response of the child to the teaching and learning situation. Beware of *too much pressure*, and be very careful that you do all you can to help the child have a positive and healthy attitude toward learning. His first learning experiences must be rewarding and filled with much more success than failure. Do not apply pressure. Keep in mind the reinforcement principle, and remember that leading positively will in the long run reach the child more

A child's feelings have a profound impact on learning

Beware of too much pressure; help your child develop a healthy attitude toward learning

deeply and effectively than efforts to drive or to punish for wrong responses.

General Educational Outcomes during the First Ten Months

During the first ten months of your child's life, you will want to systematically build his prevocabulary skills and imitative voice sounds and his visual, listening, and muscular skills. You will want to teach the child that learning can be fun and that he can be confident in his abilities.

The First Few Weeks of Life

Remember that a major purpose of early childhood education is to nurture maximum growth in intelligence. While much is not known about this process, there is good reason to believe (from research) that stimulation of mental activity at the earliest possible age is very important. Parents should be aware of this need from the time a child is a new-born infant. Varied sounds and other sensory experiences should be provided. The baby's crib should display diverse colors and patterns. Crib toys should be abundant; objects that move and toys that play music should be provided. Be sure that the crib is an active, responsive place.

Stimulation of mental activity at the earliest age is important

The baby should sit or recline in many positions during those first few weeks of life. He should have alternative locations in the home where he can see different items, shapes, and colors, both inside and outside the crib. Reaching, grasping, and kicking and also receiving auditory and visual stimulation should be provided. He should feel loved and secure and have his physical needs met promptly and regularly in response to his cries and demands. Be sure you provide stimuli for muscular development (see Crib Toys in chapter 4).

The good-natured baby also needs environmental stimulation in the home

Some babies are quiet, demanding little attention. Busy mothers can easily neglect such infants by failing to provide a stimulating and responsive environment. Often the inactive, good-natured, noncrying baby needs this environmental stimulation the most.

Activities at Sixteen Weeks of Age

By the time a baby reaches 16 weeks of age, he will have begun to show interest in matters other than feeding, sleeping, and being kept dry and clean. He will want to be held and will enjoy being propped up. Crib toys on a broader scale should come into his experience at this time. He should have his feeding and sleeping routine fairly well patterned. He should be able to follow moving objects with his eyes and be stimulated to reach for things with his hands. Tasting, touching, and reaching experiences should be provided often.

Tasting, touching, and reaching experiences should be provided

The 16-week-old child should show some emotional response to stimulating situations. He should be cooing and trying to make initial sounds other than crying. He should be stimulated to smile, even laugh aloud if he will, and to respond to all kinds of sound and motion.

It is common for mothers to demand absolute silence when the baby is taking his morning and afternoon naps. This kind of situation does not help the baby become tolerant of sudden noises or make the home a natural, normally functioning place. Teach the baby to sleep with the usual sounds around the home. He must learn to live in a world with a fairly high noise level and be able to carry on his normal

Teach the baby to sleep with the usual sounds around the home

routine while adjusting to life's circumstances. An enforced quiet and unnatural whispering or tiptoeing around the home can actually be detrimental to the infant. His sleeping and his concentration when awake must be done by blotting out distractions.

Be sure the baby is motivated to exercise arms and legs

Be sure that the baby gets exercise and a chance to move his arms and legs. If he is not active, try to stimulate him to kick and reach as much as possible. Encourage emotional response by laughing and playing with him. Give him attention, conversation, and encouragement to respond.

Activities and Capabilities of the Five- to Seven-Month-Old Infant

By the time a baby is five to seven months old (depending on each child's individual abilities), he is becoming ego centered and is demanding more attention. He prefers to be in the sitting position and struggles to be where he can see and interact with others. At this age, his sensory experiences should have increased greatly. He should be able to feel and taste and should have many objects to grasp and examine. He should demonstrate the ability to shift objects from one hand to another. Help him practice this.

Increased exposure to music and conversation should be provided

Increased exposure to music and conversation should also be provided. The infant now has more social awareness and will respond readily to stimulation. Surroundings in his crib and in other locations around the home should be of varied colors and shapes. He should have an opportunity to grasp and bang toys or his fists on his high chair or feeding table. This and other experiences should stimulate him to make vocal sounds. Encourage his vocalization as much as possible in other experiences besides crying. Try to get him to make sounds, and make a special effort to react to his vocalization.

Provide ample opportunity for the child to push up on "all fours"

The five- to seven-month-old child should be striving to get his knees under his body and to push up on "all fours." Ample opportunity for exercise in this activity must be provided. Help him to practice this feat. The extent and variety of physical activities should be intensified.

He will have begun to learn to cope with gravity from the experience of falling whenever he attempts to sit alone. In carpeted or padded areas, this type of experience should be permitted. When the five- to seven-month-old topples from a sitting position, let him struggle briefly before coming to his assistance. This will increase his physical balance and allow him to build muscular capacity. Rather than being inhibited, the infant at this age will reach to pull himself up and may even crawl. Encourage him to experiment in these endeavors.

Allow the child to build a strong muscular capacity

Activities at Ten Months of Age

Between the ages of seven and ten months, the infant will have become more restless as he tries to get on hands and knees to crawl. As he learns to move on hands and knees, a new era opens for him, and he will require some adjustments to protect him from falls and injury. Be sure to provide ample opportunity and encouragement to practice. When the baby first starts to crawl, it is the time to place brightly colored and interesting objects just beyond his grasp to encourage his reaching and to stimulate arm and leg movement. Do not frustrate him, but challenge him in a way in which he will succeed.

When your baby starts to crawl, encourage this by placing attractive objects just beyond reach

The baby at ten months of age should have developed more hand and finger coordination ability. Advanced and rapidly growing children may be able to take a few faltering steps at this age. All of these physical capabilities should be noted and encouraged.

Sensory experiences and exposure to language, music, colors, and shapes should be increased. It is time to fill his daily life with rich experiences. The toy libraries and the directions that accompany each toy will provide many stimulating and exciting experiences. Be sure to read the instructions that accompany the materials to help you make the most of these educational toys. Most toy libraries and many commercial educational toy manufacturers furnish instructions for the use of these materials.

It is time to fill the child's life with sensory experiences

Practical Application

These examples are merely a foundation. Do not feel that all of them must be introduced at the same time or that they must be presented in the sequence given below. You should develop additional, more individualized activities for your child.

Talk to the baby often during the first few weeks of life to help her develop listening skills.

Create noisemakers by putting objects in a can. Shake the can and observe the child's reactions.

Provide varied colors and change them often; keep the baby's eyes active just as soon as he can see.

From Birth to Sixteen Weeks

Many sensory experiences can be provided by the following activities:

Sounds

1. When your baby is newly born (and throughout his childhood), talk to him often. He may not appear to be listening or responding in his first few weeks of life, but he is absorbing the sounds and becoming aware so that this activity will help him develop listening skills now as well as later on.

2. When he is about six weeks old, present various sounds from different areas of the room — such as whistling or tapping gently on a windowpane with a coin, ring, or other metal object. Observe his ability to locate the source of the sound.

3. Create different noisemakers by putting objects such as a thimble, coins, or marbles into an empty can. At various intervals during the first few weeks of his life, shake the can near the infant — sometimes by his head, sometimes at his feet, sometimes behind him. Watch for signs that he is becoming alert to the presence of sound, such as interrupting what he is doing to look for the source of the noise.

Bright Colors

Many cribs are very plain and white; they are sterile and clean, but do not stimulate visual activity. Provide many varied colors and change them often to keep your baby's eyes active from the first time he is able to see.

1. Using a plain white crib sheet (or clean dish towel) for a background, sew on different bright and distinctive shapes . . . a red circle, a blue triangle, a green square, a yellow rectangle (this device will also be used later in the child's learning experiences). Place this decorated sheet over the side or back of his crib within sight of the baby. This exercise will be particularly effective when he is able to move his head freely.

2. Spread this sheet on a bed, a table, or the floor and lay the baby, stomach down, on it. As he turns his head, he will be receiving different visual stimulation.

Sew different brightly colored and distinctive shapes on a crib sheet or some other clean cloth.

Moving Objects

During the early stages of this age period (birth to eight weeks), you must place moving objects (either purchased or homemade) fairly close to the infant (within 12 inches). Moving toys can be extremely effective for your child's visual as well as mental stimulation.

1. Create moving objects for the baby to see. These can be made by painting wooden block forms (CAUTION: Always use nontoxic paint) or covering the forms with brightly colored plain or flowered fabrics. You may even want to sprinkle glitter on them. Aluminum foil wrapped tightly around objects can be used, but be sure that such items cannot be caught by the baby and the aluminum pulled off a little at a time to be inserted into his mouth.

2. Tie each object separately with pieces of string — each of varying length. (Check step 3 before proceeding.) Make sure that the objects hang free above the baby's crib and that they do not recline on his body or his bedding.

3. Place a bar across the crib with the dangling objects tied securely to it (or attach them to the ceiling). If you choose the latter, make sure that the strings are long enough to reach within 12 inches of the baby.

4. Include both plain and patterned forms. Change the moving objects frequently so that the novelty of the visual stimulation will be sustained.

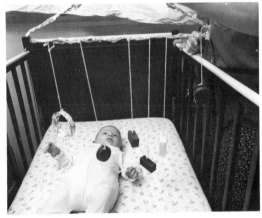

Place movable objects fairly close to the infant. These can be made from various household items.

Change the moving objects frequently so that the novelty of visual stimulation will be sustained.

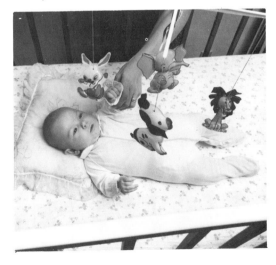

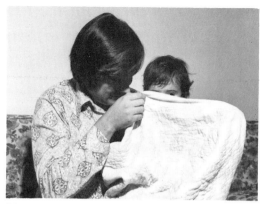

Plays games such as "peek-a-boo" with the infant; encourage him to react by using body expressions.

Place various objects in the child's hands to let him touch and feel the differences between them.

Allow your infant to touch sand, water, cereal, and other things to experience tactile sensations.

Where's the Baby?

The following activities will provide a tactile (touch) experience and will stimulate body movement as a precrawling exercise.

1. When the infant begins to move his arms and kick his legs, put him on his back and place a lightweight blanket over him. (The one you made for his visual stimulation is excellent for his exercise.)

2. Encourage him to kick and move his arms and legs by speaking to him:

"Where is [call his name]?"

"Oh, there he is."

"Peek-a-boo!"

3. If you find at any time that your baby is responding to a particular incident, use this again and again as a reinforcing experience until he tires of the activity and is ready to learn more complicated "games." Always be alert to anything that will stimulate him to use his arms and legs as "body expressions."

Something New and Different

Provide many opportunities for your baby to experience different tactile sensations.

1. Place objects in his hands, one at a time, that have a different feel and which the baby can put into his mouth . . . plastic teething rings, soft rubber toys, etc.

2. Let him touch and feel the differences between: a spool of thread and a piece of yarn, a silk scarf and a leather key case, a piece of cloth and a silver spoon. Make sure that all items are harmless to your baby.

3. Touch different parts of his body with various textures: a feather, some cotton, various blunt objects such as a closed diaper pin or a small bottle of perfume. At times, lightly pinch his skin or lovingly chuck him under the chin or on the cheek.

4. Allow your infant to touch sand, water, mud, pudding, baby cereal, etc., and provide a great deal of play activity while you are bathing him.

Sixteen Weeks to Five Months

Many parents will find it expedient to continue the activities suggested from birth to 16 weeks but will want to add other experiences such as those described below.

Sight and Sound

Moving objects for this age should provide both visual and auditory stimulation.

1. Make additional crib toys that provide sound as well as visual attraction . . . spoons or keys that clink together, hollow articles that echo as the baby hits them . . . and tie these close enough to the infant that he can reach them with his hands or feet.

2. Encourage your baby to reach and kick by speaking to him while applying these activities. When he learns that the toys make sounds as he touches them, he will attempt to move his arms and legs of his own free will.

Backward and Forward

1. Using a beach ball that is not totally inflated (somewhat soft), place the baby on his stomach over the ball.

2. Gradually roll him forward over the ball and encourage him to reach out his arms to stop himself as the ball rolls forward. As it rolls backward, let him feel the floor firmly with his feet. Practice this many times for it will enhance his balance skills later on.

3. After a period of time, you should be able to observe his anticipation of how to stop himself as he reaches or positions his arms and feet.

Here It Comes — There It Goes

1. Roll the beach ball back and forth in front of the baby so that he can follow the movements.

2. Pull, push, roll, or drag other objects in front of him . . . toy cars, large cans with bright labels, colorful blankets or fabrics, etc.

3. Related movements such as rocking your baby in a chair (you needn't have a rocking chair — the movement of your body in a plain chair to simulate the rocking motion will suffice), rolling him

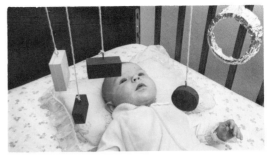

Make crib toys that have sound as well as visual attraction, hollow objects that echo when struck.

Place the baby on a semi-inflated beach ball; roll her forward; let her reach out to stop herself.

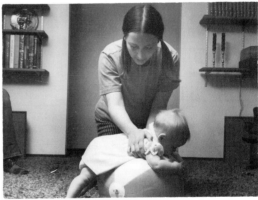

Roll the baby backward and let her feel the floor with her feet. This will enhance balance skills.

Slowly roll the beach ball back and forth so the child can follow the movement and reach for it.

Fold a blanket or bath towel lengthwise to use as a sling; hold the baby a few inches off the floor.

Move the child around the room; talk to her about various objects she sees and let them touch them.

If possible, let the infant hear the sounds made by a piano and various other musical instruments.

Take the baby outside to hear a variety of sounds . . . cars going by, an airplane, a dog barking.

from side to side on his bed or on a blanket on the floor, or playing peek-a-boo around a doorway are excellent reinforcing games for developing your child's visual and auditory perceptions.

Around the Room

1. Take one of the baby's blankets or a bath towel and fold it lengthwise on the floor.

2. Place the baby crosswise on the blanket (on his stomach). Make sure that the folded blanket is wide enough to support the baby when he is lifted.

3. Using the blanket as a "hoist," raise the baby a few inches off the floor, letting his hands and feet touch the floor.

4. Move him both forward and backward around the room.

5. As he comes near an object, talk to him about it:

"There's the chair."

"There's the television."

Let him reach out and touch them if he wants. Encourage precrawling movements of his hands and legs.

What Was That Sound?

1. When there is activity in various rooms in the house . . . preparing dinner in the kitchen, father's electric razor whirring in the bathroom, an older child practicing the piano or playing records . . . place your child where he can hear these sounds and feel that he is a part of the activity.

2. Let him listen to the radio or to records. Vary the loudness and the type of music.

3. If there is a piano or other type of musical instrument in the home, let the infant hear the sounds they make.

4. In good weather, take the baby outside where he can hear other sounds . . . cars going by, an airplane overhead, even a dog barking in the distance will attract his attention. Seek out those areas where the infant can hear many sounds.

Five to Ten Months

Continue to encourage crawling movement by lifting the baby with a blanket or towel. Progressively place more weight on his hands and feet.

I Can Move Myself!

1. As the child begins to move by himself, place objects in front of him to stimulate movement, thus enabling him to realize that he can obtain things by controlling his own movements.

2. Place different toys and other items on the floor so that the infant will have tactile contact with them . . . a soft hair brush, a clean wash cloth, a stuffed toy animal, a plastic bowl . . . and at the same time experience sensations of softness, hardness, roughness, and smoothness.

3. Place obstacles of various heights on the floor . . . a sofa cushion, a chair, some large cans . . . to encourage his standing ability as well as to teach him to realize that he must do something about the obstacle if he is to advance from here to there.

There It Is!

1. Place objects such as cans or lids on the tray of his high chair or on the table before you if you are holding him at the table. Allow him to brush the objects to the floor.

2. Encourage his curiosity by saying:

"Where did it go?"

"Oh, there it is."

3. Although he may not be interested at first, after awhile your child should begin to voluntarily look to the floor to see where the object fell.

Where Did It Go?

The following exercise provides stimulation for visual and auditory perceptions as well as for movement. This activity can be varied by the parents and used in different settings: at the dinner table, while outside the home, during the baby's bath, etc.

Place objects in front of the baby to stimulate movement and to give him tactile experiences.

Place obstacles of various heights in his path so he can learn to crawl over or go around them.

Allow him to brush objects to the floor; encourage his curiosity by asking, "Where did it go?"

Introduce different odors to your child; be sure to include both pleasant and unpleasant scents.

Increase the child's awareness of sweet and sour by giving him a chance to sample various tastes.

Provide the child with many opportunities to feel the textures of different surfaces, such as grass.

1. Place an object in front of the baby and cover it with a cloth or a cup that he can lift off.

2. Say: "Where is the [name the object]?" You may have to pull the cloth off a few times until he gets the idea and does it by himself.

This Is Strange!

1. As your child creeps and eventually walks, provide him with many opportunities to move on grass, sand, shallow water, mud. Let him feel the texture with his hands and between his toes.

2. Have him taste differently textured foods . . . dry cereals of various kinds, semisolid and solid foods, etc.

3. Introduce different scents and odors to your child. Let him smell foods, fruits and vegetables, perfume, flowers. Include both pleasant and unpleasant odors.

4. Increase your child's awareness of sweet and sour by giving him a taste of sugar or honey and then a taste of salt, lemon, or vinegar. Be sure that the sour items are a tiny taste only.

5. Provide your child with the "warm and cold" experience. Let him taste warm milk and then cold milk, or allow him to touch the warmth of his puppy's tummy and the cold of its nose. Rub an ice cube gently over his lips.

6 Learning during Ten to Eighteen Months

The child of 10 to 18 months is now reaching an age where he must have additional mind-stretching activities. He is not old enough to have formal periods of instruction, but his parents must be keenly aware of the necessity to stimulate him mentally, which must be more systematic and more deliberately planned than it was for the younger infant.

By the time the baby has reached 10 months of age, he has greater physical and mental capabilities, indicating that he is becoming a child rather than a helpless infant. He should be able to sit whenever he wants and stand with some support. It is not uncommon to see a 10-month-old baby pull himself to a standing position; a few even begin to walk at this age. Do not "push" your child to accomplish this if he is not able to do it by himself.

The 10-month-old baby is forming the capacity to respond more readily to mood and emotion. He will recognize a tone of voice that implies approval or disapproval from his parents and will be able to easily sense their moods. In short, he will be responding and participating emotionally.

At ten months, the child can recognize approval or dispproval from your voice tones

By the time the baby is 10 or 11 months of age, he will enjoy (and look forward to) playing and romping or "roughhousing." He will delight in throwing or shoving toys off tables and other places so that he can watch them fall. Because he will be very interested in many objects around him, this interest should be used for learning purposes.

At this age the baby should have an opportunity to place things inside containers and take them out again. He should be able to "stack" objects until they fall. He should be permitted to explore in the kitchen and other places where he can become acquainted with the common objects in his home. During all this, constant exposure to names of things and opportunities for him to learn their function will be very important. (Bear in mind all warnings on harmful products.)

Parents should permit their child to explore items in and places around the home

The baby is now old enough to have stories told him from pictures. These should be simple, stimulating experiences. He should have ample opportunity to learn to recognize objects in illustrations of books. This learning process will be slow at first, and much patience must be exercised.

The child should learn about animals and other forms of life

During this time the child should have an opportunity to learn about animals and other forms of life. He will be interested in dogs, cats, and other living things. Maximum exposure is very important through this particular time of his life. His experiences should be extended as broadly as possible.

Vocabulary Development

Vocabulary development is particularly important during the period from 10 to 18 months of age. By the time the child is 18 months old, he should be on the way toward building a speaking as well as a recognition vocabulary. The words he understands and is able to pronounce in his own limited way comprise his "speaking" vocabulary. The words that he understands but cannot speak comprise his "recognition" vocabulary.

Vocabulary development is vital during this stage of a child's life

The parents should endeavor to build a speaking vocabulary of approximately 20 to 40 or more words by the time the child is $1\frac{1}{2}$ years old. A recognition vocabulary of from 50 to 100 or more words is also desirable by this time. Such an attainment will be difficult for young children who seem to mature slowly. Parents should not be worried if the child falls short of this goal. It is not in the child's best interest to pressure him to reach this level. Rather, the parent should seize opportunities to teach words and to encourage and reinforce efforts to get the child to speak

Parents should teach at least twenty words to the child of this age

as many as 20 words. This can be done by giving the names of objects as the child comes into contact with them. Parts of his body, eating utensils, toys, and common objects found in his room and in the home should be mentioned frequently.

The words or sound symbols for objects found in his everyday life require cognitive power from the child's point of view to develop associations between objects and the sound produced by the vocal cords of his parents as a means of identifying these objects. By stimulating him to make these mental connections, the parent is helping to build the child's intelligence at the same time that the child is acquiring useful information and cognitive skills. Therefore, vocabulary building must be a continuous process, and parents should value the moments they spend teaching the child and watching his mental stimulation and growth.

Stimulate the child to connect the spoken names with the objects they represent

Recognition Vocabulary

Building a recognition vocabulary beyond the level of the speaking vocabulary can begin before the child develops the complex skill of making sounds with his own voice as his symbol of communication. Parents should enunciate clearly the proper word symbols for the names of objects being taught to the child. As discussed earlier in this book, it is confusing to the child to hear several names. Later in his life, he can learn that there are many names for some objects; but in these early stages of vocabulary development, the parent should use one name until maturity makes possible the understanding of other names for a particular item.

Parents should enunciate the words clearly and teach the correct names of objects

Names of Objects

Early in the child's life, the parents should repeat the correct names of objects familiar to the child. The putting on or taking off of shoes or stockings or the use of a spoon or cup at the dinner table can be the focus for vocabulary building. Many times before a child can say the word "shoes," he will get his shoes for a parent when asked to do so. Repetition of the word by the parent will actually "program" the child to understand the word "shoes."

Words can be taught as household chores are performed

Family Teamwork

Brothers and sisters or other persons having close contact with the child should understand that the parents have a regular program of early childhood growth and development in mind, and these persons should be asked to participate. They should be urged to enunciate clearly also and to use correct words for objects. Without undue repetition, the child can receive great exposure to a vocabulary that can build his intelligence and move him toward the goals we aspire to help him reach.

Conversational Stimulation

Frequent conversation should be directed at the child by all members of the family

During this period in the child's life, frequent conversation should be directed specifically to him. Short, distinct sentences should be spoken. He should have a response to his first efforts to try to speak. Jabbering incoherent sounds should be encouraged and reinforced. When he calls out, respond with words that will encourage him to use his voice more often as a means of communication and as a method for getting what he wants. Try to get him to point to

objects that he wants and to say the name of the object. Do not overdo this to the point of frustrating the child — for this will not be applying the crucial principle of reinforcement.

Seize upon every opportunity to encourage him to use his voice as a means of communication. This may start as single words and grow to simple three- or four-word sentences. The child will very likely have his own word sound for certain objects. For example, he may use the word "baba" for bottle because he cannot pronounce the proper name. Parents should avoid discouraging him from speaking by saying: "It isn't 'baba'; it is 'bottle.'" Rather, they should repeat the proper name and reinforce the child by responding to his request. Many parents make the mistake of repeating the incorrect pronunciation and adding it to their vocabulary. If spoken incorrectly often enough, the word soon seems correct to parent and child.

The chlid will very likely have a word sound for certain objects; encourage this by using the correct word

The parent must remember that, as the child's first teacher, there is a responsibility to teach correct principles and facts. This can be done at the same time that some laughing, playing, and enjoyment of learning takes place. You *can* have fun with your child and teach him correct principles. You can get down to his level and have empathy and understanding for him without being frivolously foolish in using baby talk or resorting to an incorrect principle.

Be "vocabulary conscious" through his early childhood months, but be particularly vocabulary conscious during your child's first 10 to 18 months of life. Later on in his life, you can build upon this basic vocabulary, especially during the months before he enters school. But be sure that while his basic vocabulary is being built, your child gets the benefit of mental stimulation for his growth in intellectual power. Read through this section of your book many times and do everything possible to see that the child's heritage in your home includes a maximum opportunity to develop his mind and to build a powerful vocabulary in the process.

Parents must strive to develop their child's mind and build a powerful vocabulary in the process

Building Listening Capacity and Sound Discrimination Power

The parent is an observer as well as a teacher. During these formative months of a child's life when

Parents should try
to build listening
as well as speaking
ability in their
child

his mind is particularly fertile, the parents should try
to build some listening as well as speaking ability.
(This process is discussed later in this book. It is
emphasized here to alert the parent to seize every
opportunity to teach auditory perception even at this
very early age, although we recommend a formal program when the child is more mature.)

As the child grows, he will need to distinguish
between "sound alikes" which have subtle differences;
for example, the letters *b* and *d* or *i* and *y*. He will
need to recognize many other sounds as he begins to
read and to build his basic study skills. Therefore,
during the baby's 10 to 18 months, the parent should
look for opportunities to build listening capacity and
sound discrimination power. Because children are
active and vigorous at this age, such opportunities
may be rare. When you see that your child is in an
attentive mood, whisper to him or get him to respond
in games that require hearing perception. In the educational toy library are some "sound" items to be
used with older children. Adaptations of some of these
games might be applied to the 10- to 18-month-old
child.

When the child is ready for training in listening
skills, the parent should take advantage of it. The
continuity of the entire program requires a step-by-
step, skill-building process. Each child will approach
the listening activity and respond differently. The parent should recognize this fundamental law of teaching:
Teach when there is readiness to learn. If it comes
during this period of the child's development, use the
program as discussed above. More methodology on
how to develop listening skills and sound perceptions
is found with the instructions that accompany the
educational toys in the toy library.

The child must
learn to distinguish
between "sound
alike" letters

Each child will
respond differently
to the listening
activity

Teaching Independence and Self-Reliance

Parents should be aware of the necessity to gradually teach independence and self-reliance in the home.
This should begin in the 10- to 18-month period in
the child's life. Give the child a chance to become
self-reliant; have the patience to permit him to do
things in his own slow and irregular way. Often parents do too much for the child, thereby depriving him
of the opportunity to develop his own abilities and to

build his own self-reliance. You should seldom do for a child anything he is capable of doing for himself. The only exception to this instruction should come when necessity forces you to get something done in a hurry.

In the normal routine of the home, building self-reliance should be a high-priority item. More capability will come later. If the child is to become independent, the parent must realize that to "help" is to take away potential for growth and development. Parents who make children totally and helplessly dependent upon them are depriving the youngster of development opportunities. This fact cannot be emphasized too much. The ultimate object is to raise a child who will be a happy, self-reliant, and efficient person.

Parents should let the child become self-reliant and proceed at his or her own pace

Recognition of Three Basic Geometric Shapes

When the child is between the age of 15 and 18 months, parents should expose him to recognizing circles, squares, and triangles. Educational toys that can be used to teach geometric shapes for this age group are found in the toy libraries. Be sure to become familiar with them and learn how to use them for the maximum educational benefit of your child. The instructions indicate the age level for the toys, and you should expose your child to all of the educational toys designated for the age level up to 18 months.

Teach your child the circle, square, and triangle

Additional Instructions and General Comments for Ten to Eighteen Months of Age

Although some educators argue that children of this age are so lacking in maturity that it is hard to teach them, there are some very simple things they can learn easily which will help them when they are more mature, when they have developed a vocabulary and can speak distinctly, and when their minds have been developed more fully. Educational outcomes are difficult to predict at this age.

Because the child has a limited vocabulary and an extremely short attention span, attempting to teach him presents a great challenge. Keep in mind that our program is seeking to stimulate the child to build a powerful intelligence and a good attitude toward learning. He needs a maximum opportunity to learn

Educational outcomes are difficult to predict at this age

We are not seeking
basic skills, but
the results of
strengthening the
child's intelligence

all he can during every month of the first five years of his life. If we can start him at a high level of intellectual stimulation during this younger age, he will start to build cognitive powers, and his capability for learning later on will be enhanced. We are not merely seeking the basic skills and educational outcomes, we are also seeking the results of strengthening his intelligence as a human being.

Learning experi-
ences must be
closely related to
the child's
sensory contacts

The learning experiences of the child at this time must be closely related to those things with which he has physical or sensory contact in his day-to-day encounters. For example, in building his vocabulary, be sure to include words that name parts of the body. Touch his nose and say, "This is your *nose*"; touch his foot and say, "This is your *foot*." Introduce him to the names of objects that surround him and that he can hold, touch, feel, taste, or smell. By using many of these objects and by touching, seeing, tasting, or smelling them, he has a multisensory experience that will stimulate his interest and capacity to learn.

Parents must keep
simple objectives
in mind

The child can also become familiar with actions and action words. His total environment during this period of time can be responsive and rich in learning opportunity for him. Although it will require additional work for the parents, it will nevertheless yield great dividends; but the parents must be conscious of the child's capabilities to learn and must have simple objectives in mind. Desirable objectives for the child during this period of time are as follows:

(1) To have a speaking vocabulary of approximately 20 or more words and a recognition vocabulary of approximately 50 or more words

(2) To have an initial experience with three basic geometric shapes and learn to place squares, circles, and triangles in receptacles of a similar shape

(3) To learn to sleep during relatively high noise levels in the home

(4) To have a multisensory experience with many objects around the home by being able to see, hear, or touch them or to taste or smell them and learn of their uses

(5) To learn to respond to simple instructions ("bring me your shoes"; "find your book")

(6) To learn to point to objects and say at least some of their names (an optimum number, 20 objects; a minimum, about five)

(7) To have listening experiences with initial auditory discrimination that will be useful later in learning phonics (learning the spoken value of letters and letter groups) and how to read

(8) To have experiences in assembling simple objects, such as putting lids on plastic bottles or screwing caps on empty toothpaste tubes[3]

(9) To be able to locate at least five parts of his body when asked to do so

(10) To learn to use all of the educational toys in the toy libraries that are recommended for children under 18 months of age

Attitudes toward Learning

An important objective for the parents is to learn to help the child have a positive attitude toward learning. In the process, they should help him develop a positive image of himself and feel competent in his abilities. In addition, the parents should have learned a great deal about how to teach the child. They should begin to have some idea about his strengths and limitations. They should have learned some tricks about how to hold his attention and how to interpret certain responses that he might make to the learning situation. They should be conscious of learning opportunities and be striving to make the home a powerful, responsive, learning environment for the child, where opportunities are always present to add to his growth experiences mentally as well as physically.

The parents should be as conscious of the need to nurture the child mentally and intellectually and to provide him with a balanced learning "diet" as they are to nurture him physically to make sure that he has balanced physical nutrition. These first 18 months will lay the foundation for establishing the

An important objective for the parents is to help the child have a positive attitude toward learning

---

[3]Do not be disturbed if your child does not attain this particular feat at this time.

The first eighteen months will lay the foundation for the teaching-learning relationship of parent and child

teaching and learning relationships that will help the child become intellectually alert during the remaining years of his preschool life.

In striving to reach these objectives, parents must be wise in recognizing that there are wide ranges of differences, even among very gifted children, in the time that the child is ready and interested in learning certain things and the time when he will attain certain capacities and skills. The fact that one child at one time may be considerably behind another in learning a particular skill should not alarm the parents. They must take the child as he is and work with him in a way that takes maximum advantage of his strengths and stimulates him to learn when he is ready and emotionally prepared.

The child must be emotionally ready to learn

Parents should not worry about a child's slowness, unless it departs from what is normal to such a drastic extent that it is obvious special attention is needed. In such cases, of course, specialists should be called in, and extraordinary measures may be necessary.

Few children will reach all of the objectives at the recommended time

Keep in mind that the suggested experiences in the learning outcomes are quite ideal and optimum in this program. Very few children will reach all of the objectives at the recommended time since the program is designed to stimulate and stretch the mental capacities of children having widely divergent backgrounds and abilities.

Practical Application

These examples are merely a foundation. Do not feel that all of them must be introduced at the same time or that they must be presented in the sequence given below. You should develop additional, more individualized activities for your child.

Where Am I?

1. Obtain a large packing box that your infant can crawl through. If it is more than three feet long, cut it shorter.

2. Cut out the top and bottom of the box ("tunnel") and place your infant at one end.

3. Look through the other end and encourage him to crawl through the tunnel to you.

4. Place some toys inside the tunnel and leave the box for your infant to explore at his own pace.

Make a "tunnel" from a large packing box and help the child explore this new space environment.

In It Goes!

1. Provide many containers of different sizes that will fit inside one another . . . plastic bottles, cans (with edges smoothed), plastic bowls, etc.

2. Supply an abundance of smaller objects that can be dropped into the containers . . . spools, kitchen items, blocks, rocks, etc. (Watch him constantly when he is playing with such items as rocks or marbles to be sure he doesn't put them in his mouth.)

3. You may need to demonstrate to your child what you want him to do, and through your encouragement, he will spend a great amount of time with this activity.

Provide small objects that can be dropped into containers so he can develop his coordination.

We Have That, Too!

1. The key to selecting your child's first storybooks is to relate them to his immediate surroundings.

2. An important abstract concept can start developing in your child as he sees that a picture (and as he will later realize, a word) can represent the real object.

The key to selecting the child's first storybooks is to relate them to his immediate surroundings.

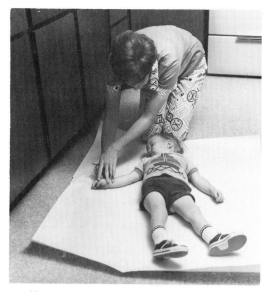

Have the child lie face up on a sheet of paper, and trace the outline of his body on the paper.

The child can assist in filling in the details such as eyes, ears, and nose. Explain the steps.

Attach the outline to cardboard; place clothing on the model so the child can view it frequently.

3. As you show your infant the pictures, incorporate the following:

"Look at the girl's shoes."

"See, here are *your* shoes."

"Show me your shoes."

"Show me the girl's shoes."

4. Do the same thing for parts of the body and for clothing, for household items, for family members, etc.

5. You may want to investigate the "scratch and smell" books to add the dimension of smell to the learning experience.

Look, That's Me!

1. Have your child lie face up on a large sheet of white paper and trace the outline of his body on the paper. (Make one more copy of the outline so that you have two.)

2. Have your child assist you in filling in the details such as eyes, ears, nose, etc. Constantly talk to him as you are adding the features.

3. Place a cardboard between the two paper outlines and attach them all together.

4. Place some clothing on the model and hang it up where your child can view it and manipulate it frequently.

5. In addition, have a full-length mirror where your child can observe himself and be instructed by you.

6. If you have photographs of your child, show them to him often to help him build his self-image.

Shapes

1. Make play dough from the recipe at the end of chapter 4. Let your child participate by handing you the measuring cup or teaspoon. Talk to him as you proceed so that he feels that he is contributing to the activity.

2. Roll the dough to a thickness of about ¼ inch. Let your child watch as you cut out the shapes. Talk to him; explain what you are doing.

3. From the rolled-out dough, cut the shapes of a circle, a square, and a triangle. Keep the outside form intact so

that the child can put the shapes back into the holes from which they came.

4. Say to your child:

"Here is a circle."

"Here is a square."

"Here is a triangle."

"Put the circle where it belongs."

5. Remember, this is an introduction to the shapes. More formal training will come later. You may want to poke a hole through the shape before it dries and then make a necklace or hanging toy for a reminder to the child.

Listen and Find It

1. Select four or five objects which have different sounds.

2. With your child in front of you, say something such as:

"Here is your truck, listen to it." (Make a whirring sound of a truck.)

"Here is your teddy bear, listen to it." (Make a growling sound of a bear.)

3. Place your child away from you with his back to you and say:

"Listen and come and pick up the thing that made the noise."

4. Increase the number of sounds and the distance, such as having him stand in another room. Be sure to give him encouragement and praise.

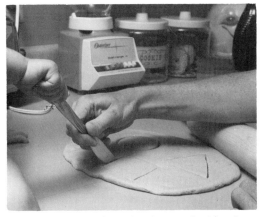

Roll play dough and cut the shapes of a triangle, a circle, and a square for the child to examine.

Let the child handle the shapes and become aware of the "holes" in the play dough where they fit.

Help the child connect sounds to the objects which make them; give him encouragement and praise.

7 Learning during Eighteen to Twenty-four Months

During the period between the age of 18 and 24 months, a child begins to attain more individuality. He learns to walk more confidently and is even able to run. As he approaches the age of two years, he begins to show much better coordination in the use of his fingers. His attention span remains short, but he will have periods of great interest and enthusiasm for learning.

At this age, the child seems to enjoy doing things exactly opposite from what his parents have in mind. For example, when asked to "come here," he will either stand still or run in the opposite direction. If the parent holds out his hand to have the child give him something, the child is likely to drop it or throw it in the opposite direction. One of the most often used words during this period of time is "NO!" This does not mean that the young child is deliberately being contrary, but merely that he has mastered a number of abilities and has a strong desire to show his independence.

The child has a short temper and is quickly frustrated at this age. He seems to have no desire to share or give. He definitely is not interested in obeying commands. He can understand many more words than he can say; but keep in mind that his understanding is also quite limited. He needs numerous outlets for his seemingly limitless physical energy; thus teaching must be wedged in around his boundless activity and

The child attains more individuality, shows opposition, and has a short temper

his desire to be constantly in motion. By the time the child passes the age of two, he has moved into another phase of activity that will not be so difficult for adults to cope with and understand.

Teaching and Learning Activities during Eighteen and Twenty-four Months of Age

The most important area of concentration during this period of the child's life must be on vocabulary development. His ability to name objects and understand word symbols for most of the things around him should be expanded as rapidly as possible. For example, by the time the child reaches age two, he should be able to locate such parts of his body as legs, knees, ankles, feet, toes, thumbs, fingers, hands, wrists, elbows, arms, shoulders, neck, chin, teeth, tongue, mouth, eyes, ears, nose, face, head, and hair. If he can locate and also name these parts of his body, he has progressed very well. But in daily contacts with the child, the parent should repeat the names of these parts of his body. As he is being dressed, the parent can ask, "What is this?" If he answers incorrectly, the parent should say, "No, it is [parent gives correct name]."

Parents should expand the child's vocabulary as rapidly as possible

It is important to have fun with the child and to help him learn the names of the parts of his body in a casual manner. This can be accomplished incidentally when the child is dressing or eating or at other times when a teaching moment presents itself.

In addition to naming the parts of the body, the child should be able to name objects in the home

In addition to naming the parts of his body, the child should learn the names of most of the items around the home with which he has regular contact. This should include eating utensils, names of items of clothing that he will wear, and common objects around the house. If he can identify these objects and also name them by the time he reaches age two, he will be doing very well in his vocabulary development.

Identifying Objects in Books

Present pictures of common objects for the child to identify

Activity with books and with pictures should be intensified during this time. Pictures of items familiar to the child should be identified on the printed page. For example, the child should look at pictures of adults and children and be able to locate parts of the body. Pictures of common objects that are known to him from his vocabulary development experience around the home should be presented for his identification.

These can come in interested telling, talking, and explaining sessions.

Using Educational Toys

Although a more serious and systematic use of educational toys begins after age two, parents should experiment with some of the games found in the educational toy library and expose the child to those experiences that are attractive and useful to him. By studying the written instructions and identifying levels of interest and ability that accompany the educational toys, parents will be able to determine a few appropriate experiences for the child even at this early stage in his development.

Experiment with games from the educational toys (borrowed, bought, or homemade)

Broadening the Range of Experiences

Children have a natural curiosity; moreover, they have a natural desire to learn and to work. Most children prefer learning activities that have real meaning rather than play that is solely for the purpose of entertainment. Children of the 18- to 24-month age span are usually very responsive to stimulating learning activities if these are presented in a challenging way that attracts the natural curiosity.

Children at this age level should begin to have a wider scope of experience. They should be taken to various places in the city and neighborhood where they can see a wide variety of things and meet increasing numbers of people. Parents should deliberately expand this range of experience after the child attains the age of 18 months.

Children at this age level should have a wider scope of experience

Building Self-Reliance

This broadening of experience should include increasing responsibility for the child. Encourage him to do everything he can for himself. Do only those things that the child is not capable of doing. Your goal should be to strive to make him self-reliant by letting him meet challenges. This should be done without frustrating the child or requiring him to do things beyond his capability. (The opposite usually happens, with parents doing entirely too much for their children at this age level. The constant expansion of the child's ability should be kept in mind, and the opportunity to gradually shift more responsibility to him should be fully utilized.)

The broadening of experience should include increasing responsibility for the child

The child should begin to feed himself or herself

The child should gradually learn to feed himself at this age in his life. Parents often neglect providing this developmental experience because they dislike the mess that is caused from the self-feeding experience. They should not, however, deprive the child of the satisfaction and fulfillment that comes from this activity. Like the other practical experiences, it should begin with the child contributing only a tiny portion of the feeding responsibility. It should continue gradually until the child is feeding himself almost independently of the parent.

Let the child get the stockings, the eating utensils, the toys

Ask the child to get his own toys that he will be using in play and learning experiences. Ask him to get his own eating utensils. See if he can put on (at least partially) his own stockings or other items of clothing during the dressing process without frustrating him or without your exerting pressure. Be naturally experimental in all of these activities.

The child will thrive on challenge and will rise to levels of expectation

Remember that your aim is to help your child become independent, original, creative, and as self-reliant as possible. During these highly formative months, start helping your child to help himself. Learning will not be superficial, and his life will be a challenging and stimulating experience if in these early months, parents are aware that the child will thrive on challenge and will rise to levels of expectation if they are presented patiently and with great thought and concern.

The Home as a Stimulating Place

During the child's age of 18 to 24 months, the parents should consider a specific place in the home where he can begin to receive some systematic learning experiences beginning at age two. The time to prepare for this is during this 18- to 24-month period.

Adjust items of equipment and furniture to the child's size

Begin to adjust many items of equipment and furniture to the size of the child. Now that he is able to walk and use his hands with greater agility, the opportunity should be provided for him to get into drawers where toys and other items are stored. Additionally, some table tops and easels should be provided at his level of height. As much as possible, the environment around him where he will be working and playing should be adjusted to a size proportionate to his needs. All of these adjustments and preparations should be made in anticipation of more serious teaching and learning that will begin when he is two years old.

Some Physical Development Activities

During this period, parents should strive to provide experiences that will develop physical coordination for the child. He should be given plastic bottles to play with. If possible, he should be helped to learn to place lids on and take them off bottles. He should be taught to place items inside and then remove them from bottles. He should have experiences in stacking these items and in steadying them so that they will not fall. A game of building a tower of some of the everyday items around the home will help to stimulate the child. In this regard, some of the objects in the toy library and around the home should be used for this type of activity.

Parents should help the child become physically coordinated

The 18-month-old child will want to scribble and mark indiscriminately on paper with crayon and pencil. He should be permitted to do this on specifically designated areas and encouraged to refrain from marking on furniture and walls. A little guidance will usually help the child to understand that there are certain items on which he is free to mark or scribble so that he can observe the results of his hand movements when using crayon and pencil. At the same time, he should learn that there are some places where he must not mark or scribble.

The child will want to scribble; teach him the proper places to do this

Parents should not attempt to teach writing at this time. The child needs more growth and maturity before he begins this activity. Be satisfied with giving him a few experiences with pencil and crayon as a form of relatively free play.

Parents should not attempt to teach writing at this time

Also during this period, the child should be given ample opportunity to carry items from one place to another in the home. In situations where the damage will not be serious, this can include the carrying of liquids. These kinds of experiences, if carried out over a period of time, will add to the maturity and confidence of the child — it will build readiness for more serious learning activities yet to come.

Teaching the child to carry liquids will add to the maturity and confidence of the child

Incidental Teaching of Concepts

During these types of physical activities, if certain concepts can be exposed for the first time, the parents should seize upon the opportunity. A simple color or number concept may be explained in an incidental way. Although children are too young to be formally taught these concepts at this time, initial exposure growing out of natural situations might be used by the parent. Other concepts such as heavy and light or hot and cold might be taught. These should be done only incidentally and only as such opportunities might develop in the day-to-day activities experienced by the child and the parent.

A simple color or number concept can be explained in an incidental way

The point is that teaching opportunities emerge from time to time, and parents should seize upon them, even if it is only to make a passing mention of a concept that may receive slight notice or cognizance from the child. Learning occurs from a host of varied and often unrelated experiences. Exposure to cognitive stimulation can occur many times in the daily routine of the child. In this regard, living and learning can be one if the parent is perceptive and alert to lead the child to learn as he encounters new experiences each day — this can happen in the grocery store, in the kitchen, in the back yard, or on the street while visiting a neighbor. The emphasis should be upon being alert to seize upon the right moment for these learning activities. These points are stressed here because the child from the 18- to 24-month period is extremely curious and is exploring so often that incidental teaching experiences abound in great number each day.

Teaching opportunities emerge from time to time; seize them

Talking to Your Child

It is vitally important that vocabulary development during this six-month period continue unabated. It is worth emphasizing again that you should be sure that you are speaking clearly and distinctly. Keep a flow of conversation moving in your daily contacts with your 18- to 24-month-old child. This is the time when he is rapidly adding to language capability. Make sure that you do your part in helping him learn to speak, listen, and understand how words add power to communicating. Help him by speaking clearly and distinctly and by adding daily to the things that he learns to identify and name. All of this will do much to help the child through learning activities that will follow in our study of early childhood education.

Keep a flow of conversation moving in your daily contacts with your child

Practical Application

These examples are merely a foundation. Do not feel that all of them must be introduced at the same time or that they must be presented in the sequence given below. You should develop additional, more individualized activities for your child.

In the following exercise, add gestures as a novel way to teach the names of items around the home.

What Do I Have?

1. Begin with some objects that are real; for example, with a spoon, stir an imaginary mixture in a bowl. (The child can see the spoon and the bowl and will be aware that you are only pretending on the mixture.) Name the items as you pick them up. Have him repeat the names as you say them.

2. Lay aside the spoon, and continue the stirring motion. Ask your child:

"What is this?" (Point to the bowl.)

He should reply:

"Bowl."

Continue the exercise by saying:

"Now I am pretending that I have something in this hand. What is it?"

He should reply:

"Spoon."

Mother: "I am pretending that I have something in my right hand. Can you tell me what it is?"

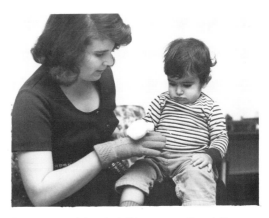

Put on an article of clothing; name it; ask the child to find and name a similar item of his own.

Vary the procedure by asking the child to name imaginary objects you indicate with hand gestures.

Describe the features of some object on the page of a book and ask the child to name the object.

When he is wrong, make a game of correcting him: "Remember, I said it had long ears, like this."

Cut odd-shaped holes in a paper and place it over the page. Ask the child to find a hidden object.

ing your teeth, picking and smelling a flower, or tasting something sour.

2. Ask him to name the object:

"Toothbrush."

"Flower."

"Lemon."

3. Ask him to get the item for you. When he returns, ask him to name it.

Listen and Show Me

1. While looking at a book together, say to your child:

"I am going to name something on this page. When you know what I am talking about, point to it."

2. Select something with which he is familiar, and begin describing it. Encourage your child to listen as you repeat the words slowly . . . "big house," "little bear," "tall boy," "long ears."

3. If when he points, he has chosen wrong, repeat the word again: "*hhh*ouse," not "*mmm*ouse." Or:

"I said it had *long* ears, and this dog has *short* ears."

Try to show the differences between what you said and what he pointed to.

4. When he points correctly, ask him to name the object. If he is unable to do so, name it for him again and have him repeat it. Take the time to refer back to the objects and have him name them again and again (reinforcement).

I Spy!

1. To add abstraction to the activity of looking at a picture book, take a sheet of plain paper the same size as the page of the book, and cut odd-shaped holes in it.

2. Place the paper with the holes in it over the picture page and say:

"Find the car that is hiding."

"Find the boy."

3. When he points to the object, remove the paper and let him see the entire

page. Praise him when he is correct; if he is wrong, discuss the differences in the objects for which you are asking and the one to which he had pointed. Repeat the exercise until he can point to the right object.

4. To advance the difficulty of the task as your child progresses in his ability to identify items through the holes, use other plain sheets of paper and make smaller holes. Do not, however, make the task *too* difficult.

5. Throughout this activity, have your child repeat the names of the objects often.

Finger Painting

1. Refer to the finger paint recipe at the end of chapter 4. When mixing the ingredients and food coloring, have your child assist you by pouring the flour into the bowl or stirring the mixture as you add the coloring. This activity alone can be a valuable learning experience.

2. Drop several tablespoonfuls of the finger paint on a large sheet of paper. If your child is hesitant to participate, begin to smooth the finger paint over the paper, and draw outlines of such things as a house, a dog, etc.

3. Add to the variety of the designs by using a damp cloth or sponge to dab on the paper, leaving a flower-like design in spots.

This activity provides an excellent opportunity for you to talk to your child and explain each step while you and he are drawing something. Be sure to display the "artwork" by hanging it on a wall with straight pins or thumbtacks.

Visiting Different Places

1. Visit outside your immediate neighborhood. Provide opportunities for your child to talk and play with other children in parks or playground areas. Visit different cultural centers (the library, a museum). You may think your baby is not old enough at this time to benefit from a museum, but he will retain some-

When the child correctly identifies the object, remove the paper to show him that he is right.

Finger painting is an excellent activity, for it provides opportunity for teaching and discussion.

Provide opportunities for the child to associate with other children at playgrounds and parks.

Visit museums, the zoo, a farm, and other places where the child can have new visual experiences. Let him set his own pace while he is very young.

thing of the experience as you return to such places while he is growing up.

2. Take frequent trips to the zoo, a farm, and other places where he can observe animal life and nature. Let your child set his own pace while he is this young — do not burden him with facts if he seems uninterested. But you can make the trips worthwhile and provide learning experiences if you point out a few details of the things he is looking at:

"See the giraffe. Look at his long neck."

"See how the monkey is opening the peanut shell."

3. Take the time to visit the pet section of large department stores and show your child the goldfish and canaries.

8 Learning during Two to Three Years

As the child reaches the age of two, we are ready to teach him systematically and to stimulate his cognitive powers. This is the time when great gains can be made if parents will thoughtfully study this book, read very carefully the directions that accompany the toy libraries, and proceed with the planned learning activities.

This also is a good time to review some of the basic principles and fundamental guidelines for teaching preschool children. Reread chapters 2 and 3 wherein the attention span, the principles of reinforcement, and other basic concepts are described so that you will have in your mind the crucial information that will help you be successful. Ask yourself how well you are doing in following the concepts that are emphasized there.

Parents should review the basic principles and guidelines for teaching preschool children

General Observations of Characteristics of Two- to Three-Year-Olds

According to most child development studies, young children, when they reach approximately 24 to 26 months of age, seem to shift to a phase in their lives when they have relatively sunny dispositions and an outgoing attitude toward others. Unlike his inclinations to be negative that came when he was about 18 months, the two-year-old usually seems to be well adjusted. At least he is more anxious to please and more willing to cooperate. However, at about 30 to 32 months of age, most children shift back tempera-

The two-year-old is anxious to please and willing to cooperate

mentally to a more contrary and antisocial disposition. Parents working in the early childhood education program will want to take full advantage of this six- to eight-month period when the child is at relative peace with the world and has a considerable amount of emotional stability, compared with the time just previous and the time coming up in a few more months.

The two-year-old child has more patience than when he was 18 months old. He is self-centered and may still have difficulty in sharing with others, but he will not be so overbearing and temperamentally unstable. He will be quite loving and affectionate at this age if he follows the norm. Therefore, he will be much easier to teach and to live with than he was a few months earlier or will be in six to eight months in the future.

Most child development textbooks caution parents to be prepared for a considerable shift in the disposition and emotional balance of the 30- to 32-month-old youngster. At this age, he is more rigid and inflexible. He is unwilling to adapt himself — domineering and demanding. He will insist upon making many decisions and will strong-mindedly demand to do things that

The two-and-a-half-year-old displays changing moods

he is incapable of doing. There will be outbursts of violent emotion if the child follows the normative behavior pattern found in most two-year-olds. At this age most children are in conflict with themselves — they will change their minds in opposite directions quickly. They will change from "I will" to "I won't" in a few seconds.

Many children at this age object to being interrupted when they are doing something. They want to persist in doing what they are doing and will refuse to change or adjust to suggestions from someone else. Childen at this age seem to be less open to change and to adaptation to new ideas, new things, and new ways of doing things.

The child will be a great challenge to the parents

The 2½-year-old will be a great challenge to parents, and this must be kept in mind as we proceed in our program of early childhood education. Parents may want to read some additional reference materials since this age has been emphasized quite heavily in the child development literature as a stormy period in the life of a very young child. The suggested references at the back of this book may be helpful.

Sometime soon after a child attains the age of three years, his disposition shifts and he will have a more cooperative and easy-going attitude toward life and toward his parents. The things to remember in working with the child during the period from two to three years of age is that the first six months of this period will be much easier than the last six. At any rate, this will be the case if the child follows the typical or normative pattern of behavior.

The three-year-old is more cooperative and has an easy-going attitude toward life and parents

Teaching Geometric Shapes

As the child reaches the age of two, he should begin to learn to recognize objects and to deal with ideas not directly related to his day-to-day living. A good approach is to reinforce his understanding of the circle, the square, and the triangle and to introduce him to other geometric shapes if he is ready for more advanced forms. Most educational toy libraries contain games (with geometric figures) that parents can play with the two-year-old. These games help the child to form a mental image of a shape and to identify it by its characteristics. Comparison of the characteristics of certain shapes helps the child to observe and draw conclusions. The instructions accompanying the toys will help parents see the value of the games as teaching tools.

Reinforce the child's knowledge of geometric shapes

Increasing Tactile Abilities

A second useful and stimulating game is played with a "guess what" bag, a small cloth bag into which the parent places a wooden geometric shape or a familiar object (some toy libraries call it a "feely bag"). The child feels the shape in the bag, and through use of his tactile sense (sense of touch), is able to point to an object sitting before him that is similar. To a parent, this may seem to be an extremely simple exercise. For a two-year-old, it can be a very rewarding and stimulating game. It will help him build his powers of mental imagery. The game can be extended to include many everyday objects such as a spoon, a comb, a pencil, and so on. By reading the directions that accompany this toy in the educational toy library, the parent can get a number of ideas on how to expand the game to add interest and enhance the variety.

The game with the "guess what" bag will increase tactile abilities and expand mental imagery

Teaching Colors

Many two-year-olds are ready to learn colors. Indeed, many children at age 18 months may find an aptitude and desire to respond to color stimulation. Again, these experiences should be presented when the parent discerns that the child is ready and interested to learn. Some perfectly normal children do not respond to color identification experiences until they are $2\frac{1}{2}$ or even three yars of age. Parents should teach when the child is ready to learn, and should not push him for a response earlier than is natural and easy for him.

Colors should be taught on a casual basis and through careful use of examples. The parents should get objects that are alike in every respect except for their colors. The parent can then say: "This is a red ball. Look at this; it is also a ball. But it is a yellow ball."

The parent can then take an object such as a ball or a block and proceed by saying: "Is this blue? No, this is not blue. It is red." It is important for a parent to present only one or two colors at a time in teaching colors. It is also important to concentrate on the most vivid colors and use the fundamental colors of black, white, red, yellow, and blue. Teach these colors first and then move to other colors.

Most children are able to grasp the concept of color quite easily. Others, however, may have some difficulty with this. Educators have found that some relatively bright children do have, for some reason or another, difficulty in grasping the concept of color. Be sure to be patient and give continuous exposure if your child is having difficulty in recognizing color. Keep in mind that you need not be in a hurry. Let the child's response tell you when to proceed.

It is particularly important to remember that the concept of color is best recognized when two familiar objects are used, with the only difference being that of color. The child will then recognize that the word "red" refers to the color and is not the name of the object. Many parents fail to realize that if they present a new object at the same time they present a new color, they are adding to the confusion and making the instruction difficult for the child. If your child is

Many two-year-olds are ready to learn colors

Colors should be taught casually and through careful use of examples

Many children grasp the concept of color easily; others find it difficult to learn

Parents should use similar objects of one color when teaching color recognition

having difficulty distinguishing between colors, use only one or two colors at a time. Crayon marks can be used; colored cellophane is a good tool. Other techniques can be devised by the creative parent in helping the child to learn color concepts.

In unusual circumstances, male children may be "color blind." This can usually be detected if the child is confusing red with other colors such as brown and green. If you detect this in your male child, have him examined by a physician to determine if he is, in fact, color blind. Color blindness in females is extremely rare.

There is a simple way to check for color blindness

Most educational toy libraries contain some games that will be useful in teaching color concepts. Use the color identification games to stimulate your child to learn his colors. Do not, however, move to the complex games requiring color knowledge until your child has learned at least the fundamental colors. You will confuse him if you are not careful in how you use some of the games in the toy libraries. Be sure to read carefully and follow instructions.

Play color identification games with toys, not complex color knowledge games

Building Listening Skills

Earlier in this manual it was suggested that the child be given some introductory experience in listening and in building skill in discriminating between sounds. More experience in building this capacity should be provided during two to three years of age. This effort should begin immediately after the child passes the age of two. Most educational toy libraries have games that are useful in building this skill. Different objects are placed in plastic containers, and the child is given an opportunity to hear the noise that the objects make when the container is shaken. He then shakes a series of containers and listens carefully until he finds an identical sound to the one he heard in the original container. Be sure to use this game as you work to teach this skill.

Parents should plan additional listening skill-building for their child

Soon after the child reaches the age of two, he should start learning the names for the letters in the alphabet, followed by some elementary phonetics. Therefore, it is important to begin at the age of two years to help the child develop the capacity to discriminate between subtle sounds. For this reason, we emphasize the use of the games in toy libraries that

The child should start learning the names of letters of the alphabet

will help build this skill prior to the time that the alphabet is taught.

Parents should play whispering games with the two-year-old child by softly whispering words that he knows well. An approach that has worked well with children of this age is to place four or five well-known objects before the child, sit behind him, and whisper the names of the objects. He should pick up the object as it is named. The parent should whisper very softly so that the child will learn to listen intently, thus helping to build listening capacity and ability to make auditory discrimination. Be sure to provide him with ample practice in listening.

Parents should teach the child to listen intently

Are You Pressuring?

Feelings and attitudes have a tremendous impact upon learning. Throughout this entire program of early childhood education, it is extremely important that we emphasize the fact that the child must not be *pressured to learn.* More important than any skill and capacity that he might develop is the need for the child to have a wholesome and positive attitude toward learning. He should look forward to the educational games that will be played with him. He should ask for opportunities to play them. Parents should not, in their eagerness to see their child advance, "push" the child to a point that he resists, cries, and objects to the whole matter of learning. This point cannot be emphasized too strongly. If you are sensitive and careful, the child's response will be wholesome, and the entire effort will be joyful.

Parents should not "push" the child to a point that he or she resists

Parents are urged to read the section in chapter 3 on reinforcement theory and how to apply it in the teaching and learning situation. Make sure that you have this fundamental principle clearly in your mind as you proceed to teach the child. Most of the learning experiences must unfold from play activity, and parents must develop the skills that make learning joyful. If the child is not learning, the fault usually does not rest with the child but with the parent. Thus if you are having problems, look to yourself first for a solution. You can be almost sure that your approach is not casual enough and that you are not making the process a pleasant experience for your child.

Most of the learning experiences must unfold from play activity

Parents who go through this program of early childhood education and succeed in making it joyful *will establish a relationship with the child that will endure for a lifetime.* On the other hand, parents who fail in this regard may do considerable damage to the attitude and emotional response of the child. Teach with understanding, in a casual manner, as you and your child work and play together. Avoid pressure . . . be relaxed. This is not to say that parents should not discipline the child and expect and get certain levels of behavior and response that are reasonable and proper. It is to emphasize that discipline and correction of behavior should usually come at a time other than the teaching and learning situation. Make the learning time the playtime in the home — it can be this and also a useful and productive endeavor.

Parents will establish a relationship with their child that will endure for a lifetime

Teaching the Function of Various Objects around the Home

Parents often take for granted the various appliances and gadgets around the home that contribute to the quality of family life. They also assume that children will learn about these appliances and machines and that there is no need to formally teach their functions. However, if we are going to accelerate the understanding of the child so that he learns as much as possible as early as possible, it is important that attention be given to some deliberate instruction. Such teaching is part of our total plan to stimulate awareness and to generate intelligence and early sensitivity in the child.

Parents should teach functions of household appliances

After the child has reached two years of age, parents should teach functions of such things as the refrigerator, washer and dryer, vacuum cleaner, kitchen range, sewing machine, heating system, water heater, pipes and plumbing system, and other appliances and gadgets that will attract the interest and generate curiosity in the child. It is important to emphasize that we are interested in teaching the *function*. More details on how they work may be left until later in the child's life. Parents should seek opportunities to expose the child to these concepts about the functions of the equipment and appliances around the home so that the child can realize that in our modern age, certain machines work for us.

Parents should use this opportunity to teach safety. The danger of playing with electric power outlets, light bulbs, and sharp objects such as knives or scissors should be taught very deliberately and carefully at this time. Simple tools such as hammers and screwdrivers can be profitably introduced to the child. When the mother or father is opening a can, the opportunity should not be missed to explain the function of the can opener. This can be particularly useful if the mother or father is opening a can to get food for the child when he is hungry. Similarly, when it gets dark and you turn on the light, explain to your child that the bulb lights up to help us see in the dark. If there is a piano in the home, the parent may want to show the child how pressing a key can make a sound and then show him the various tones on the piano. All of these experiences give depth and breadth to the intellectual exposure that the child receives.

Obviously, these teaching and learning experiences will also provide an opportunity to expand the child's vocabulary. The concept of such contrast as hot and cold can be taught while you are explaining the plumbing system. The taste of cold milk or fruit from the refrigerator provides another ideal opportunity to teach, demonstrate, and deepen the experience background of the child.

Parents should be alert to seize upon these opportunities to broaden the experience and total exposure of the child through additional concepts and ideas. Rules about touching and playing with certain appliances and conveniences around the home should be set up at this time. If properly done, this understanding and rule making will help to make the home a safe place for the child.

Practical Experiences in Helping around the Home

At the time that the child is being exposed to the uses of appliances and gadgets around the home, he should begin to learn that there is a place for the things he will be using and that he will know where to find them if they are kept in the proper place. He should, for example, be taught how to open and close drawers and in what drawers to look for objects that he will want to get. Be sure to demonstrate several

Parents should use this opportunity to teach safety

Deepen the experience background of your child

Children should learn to return toys and other items to their proper places

times how to place his fingers on the handles or knobs of drawers and how to pull them open without spilling things. Have him practice this several times and repeat constantly until you are satisfied that he has mastered this simple technique.

This is a good time to begin to teach your child how buttons and zippers work and to help him button and zip up his clothing. Board frames with cloth attached can be used to help the child practice the buttoning technique. Likewise, the function of the zipper can be taught, and the child can have the opportunity to practice on a sample item specifically designed for that purpose. A practice frame can be made, or some old clothing items can be used.

Teach your child how buttons and zippers work

At this time, the child should also be encouraged to help dress himself. Many parents make the mistake of doing too many of these things for the child for too long in his lifetime. Even if he puts his stockings on backward or with the wrong side out, he should be practicing how to do this for himself. The same thing applies to shirts, blouses, dresses, underpants, and many other items. Encourage the child to be independent and to do as much as he can for himself. Needless to say, this should not be carried too far — parents should be available to help. Avoid frustrating the child by demanding more than he can do. At first, the parents should do part and the child part of the work in the dressing and undressing process.

Encourage the child to dress herself or himself

Avoid frustrating your child by demanding more than the child can do

The lacing of shoes and the explanation that certain shoes go on certain feet can also be initiated at this time. This should be done gradually, with the child making a tiny contribution at the first experience and gradually growing in ability until he can place his feet in his shoes and even lace them up. Needless to say, it will be some time before the child will be able to tie his shoes. However, experiences in threading the laces in the shoes will be a useful developmental exercise at this time. The parent may desire to prepare an old shoe for demonstration and teaching purposes. This can be made more attractive and interesting by using some bright paint and some colored laces. Large wooden toy shoes are available on the market for teaching purposes, but an old adult-sized shoe will work as well and will cost nothing.

Threading laces in a shoe is a useful developmental exercise at this time

Learning to Handle Liquids

This is a time also to teach the child how to handle liquids and to pour from a pitcher into a cup. The parent should begin by having the child pour rice from a pitcher into a cup. After he has practiced to a point where he is adequately skilled, real liquids such as milk or water can be used instead of the rice.

Teach your child to handle a glass or cup with liquid in it

Teach the child to handle a glass or cup with liquid in it. When spills are made, have the child clean them up with your assistance. Do not do all of these clean-up tasks for him. When he is unable to do it totally by himself, participate with him and allow him to do as much as he can or as much as he is willing to do. Do not pressure the child, chastize him, or lose your patience when he spills things at the table. Work with him gradually and praise him when he successfully handles liquids without spilling. If the positive reinforcement approach is used, the child will grow in this capability and attain a valuable skill that will be useful around the home.

Vocabulary Building

As the child is learning to feed himself, the parents should also look for opportunities to teach other concepts. The idea of making things sweet by adding sugar can be taught at this time. It is easily demonstrated, and the sense of taste presents a wonderful opportunity to put over the concept. The contrasting taste of something sour (such as grapefruit) can also be taught at this time. These words and concepts added to his vocabulary will come quickly and easily in connection with the eating and self-feeding experiences.

At this time, your child should learn the concept of sweet and sour

New words such as "handle," "glass," "cup," "spout," and "pitcher" can also be taught at this time. This is a good time to teach about such items as napkins and how to fold them, to demonstrate how a sponge or a cloth can absorb liquids, to show the child how waste food is disposed of and how food can be saved for use at a later meal.

Self-help exercises will aid in building the child's vocabulary

Additional concepts can be given as the child learns such things as how to fold a napkin. He can learn how to make a triangle, a rectangle, and a square while he has an interest in folding the napkin. His attempts at doing this will be very untidy for some time. Parents should not insist on perfection; the concept and the independence are the important things.

Parents should use these experiences to teach how to set a place at the table and where the various eating utensils should go. In addition to the vocabulary teaching experiences, the child can be shown how to properly set a table and how to arrange different objects on the table. The washing and storing of dishes can be taught at this time. This can include the use of soap and the demonstration of the entire process. The child's participation should be encouraged to the extent that his maturity will permit it.

Avoiding Boredom and Pressure

In teaching all of the foreging practical skills and capabilities, the parents should be very careful to avoid letting their child become bored. Parents should remember that children of this age love repetition if it isn't overdone and should be alert to challenge the child. Do not proceed so slowly that he loses interest. On the other hand, do not move forward too quickly in introducing new materials, concepts, and skills.

> Parents should not insist on perfection

> Participation in household chores should be encouraged to the extent that maturity will permit

Adjust the exposure and teaching moment to the interest and attention span of the child

Adust the learning situation to the interest and readiness of your child

When your child is succeeding eighty percent of the time, the level of difficulty is approximately right

Observe carefully to be sure that the level of difficulty is adjusted to fit your child's ability

Adjust the exposure and the teaching moment to the interest and attention span of the child.

Be sure that your demonstrations are thoughtfully prepared and that they are presented when the interest of the child is high. Leave one item and go to another when interest is fading. Stop all teaching when it appears that the child is becoming frustrated and irritable. *Adjust the learning situation to the interest and readiness of the child.* Remember that it is important to let the child often choose what he wants to work with and to let him repeat what he is doing or permit him to stop when he so desires. Encourage the child to follow through, and teach as best you can the value of finishing a task once it is started. The skillful parent will be able to do this without pressuring or frustrating the child.

Adjusting the Level of Difficulty

Earlier in this manual we noted that the level of difficulty for the child should be adjusted in such a way that he is succeeding and doing properly those things that he is being taught most of the time. Remember that when the child is succeeding in approximately 80 percent of his attempts, the level of difficulty is approximately correct. This ensures that he is having correct responses often enough to give him adequate reinforcement and encouragement, thus giving him fulfillment in knowing that he is meeting most of his trials with success. Moreover, if approximately 20 percent of his attempts are incorrect, he is encountering a level of difficulty sufficiently challenging for the parent to know that he is continuing to learn. Be very observant to make sure that the challenge and level of difficulty are adjusted to fit these general guidelines. Since interest ebbs and flows from one day to another and from one situation to another, the parent must be constantly adapting and adjusting the learning situation to the varying circumstances. This will not be as difficult as it may seem once the parent and child are acquainted thoroughly with the temperament and technique of the other.

Teaching Counting and Number Concepts

By using the simple repetition method of instruction, parents should teach the child to say "one, two, three, four, five." The child will soon learn to repeat these numbers. After the child has mastered this capability, parents should begin to give him experiences that will connect the number that is said with the concept of the number. This is done by helping the child to understand that the last number sound that he makes with his vocal cords tells him something about a quantity of objects. This should be demonstrated, of course, by using like objects (such as three spoons).

Use the repetition method to teach the child to count

The parent may want to deepen the significance of the experience by using a "guess what" bag with three spoons in it. (If your toy library does not have this item, you may easily devise your own by preparing a small cloth bag with a draw string.) After the child has felt the bag with the three spoons, it can be opened when the interest level is high, and the parent can help the child reach in and pull out "one, two, three" spoons. This can be repeated with other numbers. Make a delightful game out of this experience, and the child will be motivated to learn to count.

Use objects found in the home to reinforce the child's counting capabilities

Parents should find incidental and casual ways to teach numbers and counting to small children. The author was interested to learn from a parent about the simple game of counting that was played by parent and child while walking up or down stairs. This is a good example of teaching while doing something else. Many number concepts can be learned by creative use of situations such as walking up a stairway and counting the steps as you go.

These number concepts should be taught gradually until the child can count to 10 and can also associate some of the numbers with the concept of the same number of objects. Parents should remember that number concepts are difficult to grasp. Since we are so thoroughly familiar with this simple concept, it is often easy for us to forget that to a person totally devoid of these concepts, a fairly high awareness is required to grasp the association of a number such as five with five objects.

Parents should remember that number concepts are hard to understand

The parent should use a number game from an educational toy library as an aid to motivating the child to learn numbers. Be sure to read the instructions carefully and follow through with the repetition and drill that is needed. These are very simple but

Most number games combine the senses of sight and touch

valuable toy experiences that can be a great aid to the child in grasping number concepts. Most number games combine the sense of sight and the sense of touch. The number games will be of additional use later in this course when numerical symbols are taught to the child.

Teaching the Child to Speak in Sentences

By the time the child has reached 2½ to three years of age, he should be able to speak in a few short sentences. Most of these should be simple statements of fact. For example, the parent may, at a particular teaching moment, ask the child to repeat the sentence: "The water is hot." The child should be urged to begin to speak in more than one- or two-word utterances. This experience can be expanded to include short and precise sentences that will help him to communicate. You will help his communicative and cognitive power as you do this.

The child should be urged to speak in more than one- or two-word utterances

When looking at pictures, the parent may want to encourage the child to say: "Dogs have four legs." This simple spoken experience can apply the power of visual discrimination and the newly developed number and counting skills, and gives the child a chance to use what he has learned.

Parents should encourage the child to answer questions as well as to ask them

Through this conversational approach to teaching, the parents should encourage the child to answer questions as well as to ask them. Begin to ask him questions and encourage responses that state a simple fact in a few short words. Strive to get simple, short-sentence answers. Be careful, however, not to frustrate expression. Encourage use of words and conversation, but do not insist on sentences if it deters the child from speaking.

Using Children's Television Shows

Encourage the child to view children's television programs

In homes where parents have access to television, the child should be encouraged to view children's TV programs as an additional enrichment experience in learning number concepts. Parents will find that the instruction in this book, the number games in the toy libraries, and TV shows for the preschool child (wherein numbers are taught) are all designed to fit well together.

Some Cautions to Follow in Teaching Numbers

Some children have great difficulty in moving from the concept of merely repeating the sounds of numbers to understanding the basic idea represented by each number sound. Parents should take time in teaching this particular skill. Be sure to approach the task in a free and easy manner. Make it a playful game. Do not be too eager. Plant an idea here and there. Repeat often and with great patience. Remember that you have a full year from age two to three years. Even if the number games are not mastered by the age of three, it will not be a serious matter.

Teach the concept of numbers with great patience

Since this is the child's first experience with mathematics, be sure that it is a pleasant and successful one. Remember the rule of reinforcement. (Remember that 80 percent of all the trials should be successful.) Avoid pressure. Teach counting and numbers only when the child is ready and eager to learn. Watch for those moments when you can stress a concept during the day-to-day activities of the child. Above all, make this first exposure to arithmetic a pleasing and reinforcing experience for the child.

Make the first exposure to arithmetic a pleasing and reinforcing experience for the child

Parents may also want to experiment with a number board game in the toy library. (Most toy libraries contain number boards.) Be sure to use this alternately with the other number games. It is a good follow-up activity that can be stimulating for the child if it is creatively introduced. For some children, one number game will be sufficient and the number board game too advanced. Parents should experiment cautiously and put the number board game away until the child has attained the age of three if the experimental introduction indicates that a later time would be more productive and useful.

Parents should experiment cautiously when presenting the number board game to the child

Practical Application

These examples are merely a foundation. Do not feel that all of them must be introduced at the same time or that they must be presented in the sequence given below. You should develop additional, more individualized activities for your child.

Touch the child's cheek with objects of various textures, such as velvet, plastic, burlap, and silk.

Take the opportunity to explain various everyday objects in terms of their unique physical qualities.

Place several textured objects in a bag and ask the child to pull out something that is "furry."

Alike or Different?

1. Collect a variety of differently textured materials such as sandpaper, velvet, plastic, burlap, silk, cotton, sponge, and other materials which are rough, smooth, bumpy, grooved, or have other distinguishing features.

2. Use these materials to teach concepts of: rough and smooth, soft and hard, and other similarities and differences which can be seen or felt.

3. Say to the child:

"This one is smooth, feel it" (plastic).

"This is rough, feel it" (sandpaper).

"Hand me the rough one."

"Can you find something else that is rough?"

"This is soft" (cotton).

"This is hard" (wood).

"Show me something else that is soft."

4. When you feel that your child understands the concept, remove all the materials from his sight. Next, place a few of them in a bag and tell him:

"Pull out something that is furry."

"Pull out something that is rough."

What Touched Me?

This exercise is particularly good since it incorporates something already known to the child — the parts of his body — and his successful responses will be reinforcing to him.

1. Begin by showing your child sets of two different items such as *cotton* and a *pencil*, a *hair curler* and a *cleansing tissue*. With the items, touch him on parts of his body . . . *cotton* on the *nose* and a *pencil* on the *leg*, or a *hair curler* on the back of his *neck* and the crumpled *tissue* rubbed on his *leg*.

2. Have him close his eyes and guess what touched him as you rub the *tissue* on his *arm* and the *pencil* on his *neck*, or the *hair curler* on his *ear* and the *cotton* on his *hand*. (Notice that the sequence has been varied in this step. See if he is aware of this fact. If not, start again with step 1 for reinforcement.)

3. Now that he has mastered telling you which item touched him, have him tell you which part of his body you have touched. (Vary the sequence once more. Continue this exercise until you are sure your child understands the concept of feeling while not being able to see the items.)

Guess What!

1. Collect a variety of familiar household items such as eating utensils, a comb, a toothbrush, soap, a shoe lace, and other items which can be easily handled by a young child.

2. Without letting him see which item you choose, place one of them in a paper sack and say:

> "Put your hand in the sack and feel what is in there."

Do not let him draw the item from the sack. Then say:

> "*Show* me what you do with it."

> "*Tell* me what you do with it."

3. Ask other questions such as:

> "Does it belong to Daddy?"

> "Does it go in the kitchen?"

Show the child different objects; then have her close her eyes and guess which one is touching her.

Place a familiar object in a bag and have the child identify it by touch to develop tactile ability.

For variation, ask the child to identify the item in the bag and then demonstrate how it can be used.

Increase the difficulty by adding more objects to the bag and asking the child to select one of them.

Place several edible items on the table and ask the child to describe their appearance and taste.

Have the child close her eyes; place items in her mouth; ask her to identify them by taste and feel.

"Who uses the [name the item]?"

"Tell me about it."

He may not be able to tell you more than a word or two, but encourage him by asking:

"Is it soft?"

"Is it hard?"

4. Increase the difficulty by adding more and more objects to the sack, and have him select the one you describe.

5. Think of as many words as you know he understands to describe the object . . . ownership, size, weight, use, and other characteristics . . . and get him to respond, such as:

"Daddy's comb."

"Little car."

Things to Eat

1. Collect a variety of things to eat which can be stored in a small plastic bag or container. Include such things as breakfast cereals, chocolate chips, various shaped candy, marshmallows, raisins, etc.

2. Place one of these edibles in front of your child and ask:

"What color is it?"

"Is it soft or hard?"

"What do you do with it?"

"Here, put one in your mouth."

"Feel how ...... and ...... it is."

Supply your own descriptive words: soft, cold, etc.

3. Introduce other edibles until the child is familiar with the characteristics of each. Then say the following:

"Here is a raisin, a chocolate chip, and a marshmallow."

Place these in front of your child and say:

"I'm holding another one of these in my hand and I'm going to put it in your mouth."

Have him close his eyes, and tell him:

> "Feel it with your tongue. Now point to the one on the table that is like the one in your mouth."

If he succeeds, say:

> "That's right. Now, let's try another."

4. Vary this activity by having your child select an item and put it in *his* mouth without letting *you* see it and then ask him:

> "Is it crunchy?"

> "Is it hard?"

> "Do we eat it for breakfast?"

Attempt to incorporate other characteristics with which he is familiar, such as color, shape, use, etc.

Geometric Shapes

1. Make several circles, squares, triangles, and rectangles from paper, cardboard, or other material which will hold its form.

2. Introduce one shape at a time until the child can readily identify it. When he has learned all of them, mix them together and have him sort them.

3. Continue this activity until your child is not only able to point to a specific shape when you instruct him, but is also able to give you the name.

4. Cut away portions of some of the shapes so that the child will learn to identify a shape when all of it is not present.

Teaching Colors

1. Take two different colors of play dough and make duplicate objects from each color, such as a red and a blue snake, dog, or ball.

2. Say to the child:

> "Here are two dogs."

> "This is a red dog and this is a blue dog."

> "Show me the blue dog."

Vary the approach to teach concepts of texture, color, shape, and use. Don't make it too difficult.

Introduce geometric shapes one at a time until the child is able to name and identify each of them.

The child will eventually be able to sort out the shapes or to gather them by name when he is asked.

When teaching colors, try to use similar objects of different colors to avoid possible confusion.

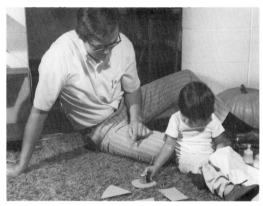

Begin to combine teaching goals. Ask the child to place blue pegs on the circle, red on the triangle.

Review colors often with the child, asking him to distinguish colors of play objects and other items.

Repeat this activity, using different objects.

3. Vary this activity by telling your child:

"Put the cup over the blue dog."

"Place the red ball on the floor."

"Hand me the blue snake."

"Make another yellow ball."

4. After your child has learned a few colors by pointing to them when you request it, begin to have him say the names of the colors. Ask him:

"What color is the dog?"

"What color is the snake?"

5. Review colors with your child constantly by asking him to use his understanding of color to distinguish the color of clothing, foods, cars, etc. Encourage his efforts (reinforcement) by saying:

"Hey. You know that color, don't you?"

9 Additional Learning for Two- and Three-Year-Olds

From the age of two to three years, the child has an amazing capacity for learning. The challenge for the parent is to assist and stimulate the child to build his intelligence. This 12-month span is truly the "golden opportunity" to help the child build cognitive power that will be with him the remainder of his life. Be especially careful to make all experience a happy time of teaching and learning; use every day of this 12-month period to maximum advantage. Use the educational toys to enrich the learning environment in the home and everything in the home in such a way that it will make the total environment surrounding the child a learning and growing laboratory. Keep in mind that you are working with a highly absorbent mind. Your finest opportunity to teach your child is when he is eager and responsive.

The instructions that follow will help you to teach abstract concepts and ideas, the names for the letters of the alphabet, relationships, and positions. Study the material carefully and prepare to use the suggestions and instructions to the maximum advantage of the child.

Teaching Names of Letters

The learning of the letters in the alphabet will likely be the most difficult task that your child has faced so far in his early childhood education career. Parents should begin by teaching capital letters only; lower-case (small) letters will be taught later.

At this age, the child has an amazing capacity for learning; stimulate the child to build a great intelligence

Learning the letters of the alphabet is likely the most difficult task your child has met so far

Children learn the
letters of the
alphabet by sight
characteristics

The parent should remember that the child has been experiencing since birth how to recognize and name different objects in his environment. He has looked at different parts of his body and learned how to name them. He has looked at common objects around the home and learned how to identify them. In like manner, he will learn (by sight characteristics) the letters of the alphabet. He will not know the function of letters in the alphabet at this early stage in his development. But if he can recognize that the letter *A* is called "A" and has certain physical features by which it can be identified, he will have attained a first step in mastering this skill. Experience has indicated that the child may be ready to learn the letters of the alphabet at two years of age. Some, however, may not begin until $2\frac{1}{2}$ years of age; some children may require additional time — and this instruction could easily be delayed until the child is three years of age.

Casually expose the
child to letters
and move along as
he or she learns

Parents should begin teaching when the child is ready for such abstract learning. Do not be overly anxious about this. Casually expose the child and move along as he learns. At the outset, the lessons should be very short. Usually a five-minute exposure to letters will be sufficient. It is better to start with a very minimal exposure time and to stop when interest is still high.

Using Television Programs and Toy Libraries

Parents should use
the alphabet board
and television pro-
grams to enrich the
child's learning

The alphabet board found in most toy libraries will be useful in teaching the names of letters. In addition, television programs, aimed at the preschool youngster, can provide extremely valuable enrichment material. The Children's Television Workshop's "Sesame Street" series presents in an ingenious and stimulating manner the concepts of letters. If the child has been viewing programs of this type for some months, the parent may need to adjust the instruction level to the child's competence — for he may already have learned several letters' names.

In teaching the names of the letters of the alphabet, be sure to refer only to the *names* and avoid teaching the *sounds* that letters can make. Such TV fare as the "pop up" commercials on children's cartoons teach the various sound of vowels, but this is aimed at the child old enough to go to school where such abstract concepts are taught to the older child. Unless you find that your preschool child is being confused by such programs, ignore these TV lessons, and your child will do the same. Presentation of both name and sound concepts will be confusing to him at this age.

Teach only the names, not the sounds of letters

Parents should not commit the common mistake of beginning by teaching that "*A* is the word 'apple.' " You should teach the simple concept that *A* is "A" because it is shaped like the letter *A*. The child is not ready to read words, and you will confuse him if you associate "apple" with the letter *A* because he will not understand that "apple" is an abstract symbol representing a food he eats. Avoid confusion by simply teaching the letter as such and the name for it.

The child is not ready to read words at this time

Strategy of Teaching

Teach three or four letters at a time in each session. Repeat and review often. Begin a new lesson by reviewing what was taught the time before. Devise games with the alphabet board from a toy library. Do all you can to play games as you teach the alphabet. This will be a particularly difficult learning experience for the child, and the parent must move along very slowly. The lessons should be extremely brief but repetitious. There should not be long gaps of several days between the lessons. Try to arrange a small amount of exposure each day.

Parents should do all they can to play games as they teach the alphabet

As you draw the letters on the paper or as you show the letters from the alphabet board game, point out the characteristics of the letters by showing the different parts and by indicating how one letter differs from another. For example, show how the capital letters *C* and *D* have part of a circle and show how they are different as well as alike. The same thing can be done with the letters *F* and *E*, and so forth. Think through different ways to teach identifying characteristics of each letter.

Point out how the letters differ from each other in sound and structure

Remember that it is easy for children to confuse letters because many are similar. For example, *X* looks much like *K* to the unpracticed eye; *R* resembles *B*. Parents should anticipate trouble with some of these types of letters and show the subtle differences. You may point out, for example, that *R* has a "leg" that is "straight" but *B*'s is "round" or "bent." This can be illustrated with chalk on a chalkboard or with crayon or pencil on paper. Be very patient and teach the letters slowly, gradually, and systematically. Think through how similar appearing letters could be confusing, and point out the differences in them. Use such terms as "humps," "bars," "curves," and "legs" in describing different characteristics of letters. By doing this, you can indicate that the letter *S* has two curves in it. You can show that the letter *H* has two legs with a bar connecting them. You can show that the letters *C* and *G* look similar and that they sound much alike, but you might indicate that *G* has a short bar on it to distinguish it from *C*. Some teachers indicate that *G* has a "shelf" on it. Continue to teach as you point out these differences.

Take extra time to show the differences in letters that resemble each other

Be sure to repeat and review. As you go through some practice and drill, try to make an interesting game out of your activity. As you look at books around the home and at signs and billboards when you are driving in the car, encourage your child to practice looking for letters. This will help to keep him interested and will call his attention to the fact that he is surrounded with these letters that have messages for people.

Parents should be sure to repeat and review what has already been taught

Teaching Lower-Case Letters

As you begin to teach lower-case (small) letters, it will become obvious that nearly half of these have the same difficult learning characteristics as capital letters. The letters that will take some drill to teach are the following: *a*, *b*, *d*, *e*, *g*, *h*, *l*, *n*, *q*, and *r*. These letters should be taught with the same precision that the capital letters were taught. Some lower-case letters (such as *b* and *d*) are so much alike that it may take a long time for the child to master the subtle differences. Do not spend too much time on them. Try to teach the differences and move along to other, more interesting things.

Teach lower-case letters with the same precision that capital letters were taught

It will be a profitable review and practice experience to have the child now look for both capitalized and lower-case letters as he looks at books, signs, and posters. When traveling in the car, you may play a game by looking for letters on signposts, etc. Be sure to use all of the opportunities in the toy library to

Have your child now look for both capitalized and lower-case letters in books, signs, and posters

reinforce the instruction offered in teaching the names of the letters in the alphabet. Also be sure to avoid teaching the sounds that they make at this particular time. This will come later in our course of instruction.

Goal in Teaching Letters

The goal of our program of instruction during the period from two to three years is to have the child be able to identify all of the capital letters and almost all of the small letters in the alphabet by the time he is three years old. It may be possible, however, that the child will not be able to distinguish between the small letters *b* and *d* or *p* and *q*. Parents should avoid spending too much time on this problem. The ability to distinguish between these subtle differences will come later for most children.

The goal is to have the child recognize all capital and some small letters by the time he is three years old

Children who are constant viewers of such programs as "Sesame Street" will likely learn the letters of the alphabet more rapidly and may be ready to move on earlier than age three to additional learnings that will be suggested for the period of time from three to four years. Parents are advised to let the child move along as rapidly as possible. But you must avoid being overly ambitious and avoid pushing when helping your child master these basic concepts.

Be sure to bring variety into the instruction. Invent different games and be prepared to use the games suggested in the toy library. Look for teaching opportunities and for chances to remind and review in your day-to-day experiences with the child.

Parents should try to bring variety into the instruction

Reading, Telling Stories, and Becoming Familiar with Books

Most children of this age enjoy looking at pictures in well-illustrated books. They enjoy bedtime stories. From the age of two years, children should be read to regularly. Be sure that you provide your child with this opportunity to share with you the exciting world of reading and the joy of learning and discovering through the printed page.

Children should be read to regularly

It is important that the parent look for opportunities for vocabulary building during this time. It is also important that some of the illustrations in the book be called to the attention of the child. Be sure to show the child some of the details in the illustra-

Show your child some of the details in pictures; help build the child's vocabulary at the same time

tions and explain to him how these pictures depict some part of the story that is read to him. After the book or story becomes familiar, give the child an opportunity to explain it to you. Draw him out with leading questions. Ask questions that will help the child identify with the story and become a part of it. Teach him to be observant and to watch closely for meanings in illustrations that are familiar to him and will help him have identity with the story. The ability to get meaning from illustrations and pictures will be useful to the child when he enters school.

Without trying to teach reading at this time, instill in the child an understanding of the concept of reading

As the child is learning the alphabet, the parents should explain that the words being read to the child are made up of these 26 letters. Without attempting to teach any reading at this time, instill in your child an undersanding of the concept of reading; it will be important to him in future years. Use this reading time as a period when some of the other learning activities can be supplemented and reinforced. Watch for number-teaching opportunities and for correlation of other subject matter during reading and story time.

Teaching Descriptive Words and Words to Help the Child Follow Directions

Words that describe and compare should be taught

Another important component of the early childhood education curriculum is for the parent to orally teach comparative and descriptive words and those words that will help the child understand and follow directions. Such concepts as big and little, fast and slow, hot and cold, soft and hard, tall and short, right and left, inside and outside, on and off, in front of and back of, above and below, first and last, and other sets of words that provide comparative and descriptive vocabulary power should be taught.

Those words that have to do with position relationships, size relationships, and location can be easily taught from the games provided in most educational toy libraries. Read the directions that accompany the toys carefully, and follow the suggested procedures. Most of these have been developed as a result of considerable research. Parents should proceed to teach with confidence, according to the techniques contained in the directions accompanying the toys.

These vocabulary concepts about comparative and descriptive words should be worked in with other instructional activities throughout the 12-month period. Try, however, to avoid teaching too many of these words at a time. By using a gradual approach over a span of 12 months, you will be able to make considerable progress, and most children will have an understanding of these words by the time they reach the age of three.

Avoid teaching too many words at a time

Additional Instruction in Listening Skills

It is important that parents continue to teach listening skills to the child during this period of his life. Use the sound discrimination game in the toy library often. Try to devise other drills that will be interesting and fun for the child and will help him to have auditory discerning powers. This skill will be useful when he moves into phonics in the elementary school reading program. Be sure to work on this skill and do all you can to teach your child to recognize the subtle differences in sounds such as *F* and *S*.

Devise games for building auditory discerning powers

Review of Reinforcement Theory

Parents should review often the material contained in chapter 3 on the educational value and power of reinforcement. As you move along to this stage in the child's development, it is particularly important that he have positive, reinforcing, joyful experiences in learning. This vital educational principle cannot be emphasized too strongly. It is recommended that you review the basic instructions on reinforcement; think about the strategy you have been using. Think through some additional strategies that may help to improve your application of the reinforcement theory. Make sure that your child is enjoying his learning experiences by being casual and by avoiding the pressure of formal teaching as it is traditionally practiced. Be relaxed, and teach as you work and play together.

It is particularly important that the child have positive, reinforcing, joyful experiences in learning at this time

Need for Commitment of Time from Parents

It may seem that the early childhood education program recommended in this book requires a great amount of time from the parents. If you develop the ability to teach while you perform other tasks, the act of teaching will not seem so demanding. It is important, however, for parents to persevere in systematically helping the child build a more powerful

If you develop the ability to teach while you perform other tasks, the act of teaching will not seem so demanding

intelligence during these years when his mental capacity is so malleable. Parents should remember that they are giving the child a priceless gift when they help him build an apt and powerful intellect. If this is done early in the child's life and if he is given every possible opportunity to expand his cognitive powers, the parents will be rewarded in the knowledge that the child is systematically gaining confidence and gradually acquiring skills and capabilities that far exceed the infant not involved in such an active and dynamic learning environment. The time spent in studying the contents of this book and the time spent in learning how to use the educational toys properly will be well worth the effort. Parents are urged to give the child the *total* program. They should persist in their efforts each day and strive for the patience and insight necessary for success in teaching the very young.

Parents should remember that they are giving the child a priceless gift when they help build an apt and powerful intellect

Parents are urged to give the total program of this book

Individual Differences

Because there are great differences in the growth patterns of children, it is difficult for a book of this type to take into account the broad span of abilities and readiness at all age levels. Some children will be able to progress faster than is recommended in the book; others may move along more slowly. Some children — in fact many children — have intermittent patterns of tediously slow progress followed by a great surge of interest and learning growth.

Some children progress faster than others

Parents should accept the child as he is and work with him on whatever level of ability he may have at any particular time in his life. They should not be alarmed if the child is behind the recommended levels of accomplishment contained in this book. The levels of skill are very challenging, and some children will not be ready at the suggested age for a specific activity. In almost all cases, if the parent is patient and understanding, the slow phases of learning will pass and rewarding learning experiences will unfold later in the child's life.

Parents should accept the child as he or she is and not be alarmed if the child is behind in the recommended levels

Practical Application

These examples are merely a foundation. Do not feel that all of them must be introduced at the same time or that they must be presented in the sequence given below. You should develop additional, more individualized activities for your child.

Alphabet Games

1. Cut two sets of the letters of the alphabet from magazines, newspapers, etc. Hide a few of the letters in conspicuous places. Show your child a letter and have him find the other that is like it.

2. Have your child assist in forming the letters with beans on paste or glue, or with finger paint, play dough, paper and pencil, or crayon. Take the time to explain the features of a letter as it is being formed.

Have the child assist in forming letters with beans or other media. Explain the features of letters.

3. Place three or four letters in front of your child. Examine each letter together. Explain to him that you are going to cover a letter with your hand (cup, paper), and ask him to tell you the letter you covered. Reverse the roles and have him cover the letter and let you reply.

4. Combine several concepts by having the alphabet before your child and asking:

"Which letter comes fifth?"

"Which letter comes after L?"

"Which letter comes before C?"

"$A, B, C, D, \ldots$"

He should supply the letter E to the last sentence.

Using only three or four letters at one time, ask the child to cover the letters as you name them.

The concept of capital and lower-case letters is a difficult one. Introduce it slowly and patiently.

Same but Different Letters

1. When your child has learned the capital (upper-case) letters, teach him the lower-case letters.

2. Explain by saying:

"This is a capital A and this is a small a. They have the same name, but are used differently."

While reading to the child, point out how capital and lower-case letters differ and how they are used.

The child should become aware of sounds. Identify them for him whenever new kinds of sound are heard.

Sound consciousness can be increased by even such a simple device as attaching a bell to the shoe.

3. After he has learned three or four letters, scramble them and then let him match the upper- and lower-case pairs.

4. While reading to your child, point out where upper- and lower-case letters are used.

What Do You Hear?

You may want to schedule the following activity when the neighborhood is busy and providing many different sounds.

1. While sitting quietly outdoors with your child, call his attention to different sounds and identify them for him:

> "Listen. Can you hear the bird?"

> "I can hear an airplane, can you?"

> "Did you hear the dog bark?"

2. Ask him to listen for other sounds and tell you what he hears.

What Comes Next?

The following exercise will build a more attentive listening capacity in your child.

1. Begin a sentence for your child to see if he can come up with the right word:

> "I button my ...."

> "I want a glass of ...."

> "We live in a ...."

2. Think of other sentences to which he can relate and which he can complete.

3. If you have taught him nursery rhymes or he recognizes a familiar song, say part of a phrase and let him complete it.

That's Not Right!

1. Add some nonsense or an error when reciting a nursery rhyme or some situational activity and see if your child can catch the mistake.

2. Say such things as:

"Jack and *Mary* [Jill] went up the hill . . ."

"Isn't this milk *hot* [cold]?"

"Look at that *blue* [red] car."

3. Make the errors on concepts with which your child is very familiar so that you do not confuse him. Make sure he *knows* the right answer before presenting a wrong or nonsensical word.

Listening capacity can be encouraged by playing simple word games: "This is how I button my _____."

Talk to the child often, and give him opportunity to express himself. Make occasional "errors" so that he can correct you: "Isn't the milk hot?"

10 Learning during Three to Four Years

Most authorities on early child development consider age three to be a delightful stage in the life of a child. He has outgrown the negative, resisting behavior typical of the 2½-year-old. He is becoming somewhat less self-centered and domineering in his behavior, and is more willing to give and take and to cooperate.

The physical capabilities of the three-year-old allow easy movement and quick actions. He can successfully play many games that were baffling and difficult for him six months earlier. This increased physical capability adds confidence and helps the child gain more satisfaction and release from his tensions through vigorous physical activity and play. This same capability may lead him away from interest in the quiet type of activity necessary for learning.

The three-year-old is an extremely social person and will want to engage in activities and conversation with others. His language capability adds to the enjoyment he gets from this. He is learning new words very rapidly and is trying them out regularly.

Changing Behavior

Typical of the ups and downs of childhood is the change in the child when he reaches approximately 3½ years of age. At this time, he shifts his behavior pattern considerably; another period of uncertainty and inability enters his life. Some children begin to show signs of stuttering at the age of 3½ . . . other

The physical capabilities of the three-year-old allow easy movement and quick actions

The three-year-old is an extremely social child who is learning new words rapidly

At this time, the child shifts his or her behavioral patterns

fears creep into the child's mind and are manifested in his behavior. He will seem to be more awkward and uncertain of his physical capabilities than he was a short time earlier. Other activities irritating to parents such as nail biting, nose picking, thumb sucking, and twisting of facial expressions often appear at 3½ years of age.

Emotional extremes of the child need patience and understanding from the parents

The child's uncertainty causes him to be jealous and at times belligerent toward parents and other members of the family. His emotional extremes and insecurity need patience and understanding. These facts of human growth and development should be kept in mind as parents proceed with the program of home-based, early childhood education. The child's need for additional affection and security should be provided by the parents, and teaching and learning activities should be adjusted to this stormy period in the child's life-cycle of growing.

Parents should try to understand the phases and cycles that run through the growth patterns of the very young

There is no doubt that the feelings and emotional responses of children influence learning. Although space limitations in this book make it impossible to detail the *physical* and *emotional* development of the child, parents should understand the phases and cycles that run through the growth pattern of the very young. As we focus our concern on the child's mind, we must remember that our total concern is the all-important education of the child. Parents who have the time and the added interest will benefit from reading a good child development text if information in depth is desired beyond the introductory facts presented in this book. Additional references are suggested at the back of this book.

Teaching the Concept of Time

The three-year-old should begin to form some ideas about time and how we measure and live by the clock and the calendar. Parents should begin to talk about the seven days in the week and to teach the child to pronounce the names of the days and repeat them in the proper sequential order. Although he is not ready to learn to tell time, he should know that we have clocks and watches that help us to meet our commitments and to do things when they should be done.

Teach the days of the week and the time-of-day concept casually but carefully

The child should learn that there are seven days in a week and that a day relates to daylight and darkness that come regularly one after the other. He should learn that there are certain things we do in a regular and routine manner . . . that some days are for some functions and others are for other functions. He can learn from those days when his father goes to work and from other days in the week some concepts about time and routine that the family follows.

The child should also be taught the concept of yesterday, tomorrow, and today. He should know, for example, that tomorrow is always the day that follows today. If he has learned the names of the days of the week in proper order, he will be able to conclude that the terms "yesterday" and "tomorrow" are also specific days of the week, depending upon what today is.

Focus extra attention on teaching the concept of today, tomorrow, and yesterday

For children having difficulty understanding what today, tomorrow, and yesterday mean, parents should devise a method of giving concrete illustrations. By placing cardboard squares (with the names of the seven days of the week printed on them) on the floor, the parent can ask the child to stand on one square. Then if the child has learned to repeat the names of the days consecutively and in proper sequence, it will be easy for him to look behind himself and conclude that yesterday was Thursday because he is standing on today which is Friday.

Parents may want to follow this teaching and learning experience by teaching the months in the year; however, these lessons can be delayed until the child has more maturity and can more readily grasp the concept. (It will be easier for him to understand about days because they come and go often enough to become part of his awareness.) Because months of the year do not repeat in a cycle, from the child's point of view, it is harder for this concept to be taught. The response should let the parent know if the child is understanding the idea of the months of the year.

If your child is ready, teach the names of the months

Teaching and Learning Experiences about Numbers

As parents teach additional arithmetic skills to the child three to four years of age, they should remember that abstract thinking is very difficult for him at this time. Since mathematics is almost pure logic, methods must be devised to illustrate through

Since mathematics is pure logic, methods must be devised to illustrate these concepts

the manipulation of actual objects the mathematical concepts that are being introduced to the child.

Most educational toy libraries have games designed as teaching aids to provide actual visual and manipulative experiences in number concepts. These toys should come into increasingly frequent use during the period of three to four years in the total early childhood educational program.

Building Cognitive Powers

The experiences in gaining mathematical concepts early in life will be extremely valuable to the child. Parents should keep in mind that our primary purpose is to build a more powerful intelligence. The gain from pursuing the knowledge and attaining the skills in this early childhood educational program will be of more worth than the knowledge itself. This cognitive power is developed through the experience that comes from acquiring knowledge.

Cognitive power is developed through the experience that comes from acquiring knowledge

It would be much easier, from the point of view of the child's simply gaining knowledge, to wait for him to become more mature before teaching him some of the abstract facts of mathematics. Such experience would occur after he has passed the age of six. However, this would be too late for the parents to take full advantage of nurturing his basic intelligence. Keep in mind that research has proved that more than 60 percent of the intelligence a human has at maturity is formed *prior to the time he enters school*. It is the initial care and the systematic development of this intelligence which we seek to instill in the parents with this program of early childhood education. Moreover, knowledge and skill are valuable to the child as he enters his school experience.

More than eighty percent of the intelligence that a human has at maturity is formed prior to the time he enters school

Understanding Numbers

From the time a child is three to four years old, be sure to count to him so that he *understands*. Children who can repeat the names of numbers in sequential order may not be able to count with understanding. Parents should make sure that this ability has been acquired from the learning experiences given to the child.

Be sure to count to the child so that he or she understands

Groups of identical objects should be counted together by the parent and the child in order to gain this skill. The important thing to remember is that the child must know that when he is counting a group of objects, the last number he repeats in his counting will tell him something about all of the objects he is counting. If, for example, he is counting to six, he should remember that the sixth square or circle tells him that the one immediately preceding it was five and that the first one he touched and counted was one. This seems simple to a parent, but it is a difficult concept for a young child to grasp.

Over very brief periods of time lasting not more than five or six minutes, the parents should work regularly and systematically with the child in helping him with his knowledge of numbers. Be sure to ask questions and participate in the experience in a way that will keep the child interested and excited. Play the games from the toy libraries that attract him the most. Be patient and do not assume too quickly that the child has understood what you are trying to teach. Children are skilled at mimicry, and parents are surprised many times to find that what they have taught as a matter of logic was only reiterated by the child by his repeating or mimicking what the parent said.

Do not assume too quickly that your child understands what you are trying to teach about numbers

In difficult circumstances, it may be helpful to place objects to be counted on the living room floor with six inches to a foot of space between them. The spacing should be even, but the objects should be well spaced and systematically arranged in a way that will not confuse the child.

The child should learn to count up to 10 objects and to have the actual understanding of the concept "ten" when he counts out 10 objects. Be careful about the natural inclination of a child to count one object more than once. He needs to follow certain rules of procedure established by the parent in all of the counting games. Toys from the educational toy libraries are useful in this need to make sure that understanding and not mimicry has been attained.

Watching the Attention Span

Parents should remember that the attention span of the three-year-old is not long. Also, he can become engrossed in something besides the mathematical concept very easily. If, for example, you have him picking up and counting squares or circles, the child may be-

The attention span of the three-year-old is not long

come absorbed in manipulating the blocks or other objects that you are using. When actual objects are used from the toy library or from other sources, it is often wise to play with the child for a while to help him become familiar with objects as such before having him shift to the counting experience.

Additional Mastery of Numbers

After the child has learned how to count and has the meaning behind what he is doing, he is ready to learn some other important concepts about numbers. He should be given a certain number of objects and asked "How many?" Then one object should be taken away and he should be asked "Now, how many?" This should be followed by the practice of giving him a large number of objects and saying "Give me three." He needs to learn the rule that he stops after he has counted to the number three. This will take some time and will not be as easily mastered by the child as many parents think. Considerable repetition will be useful to the child and should be provided when the child is anxious and ready to play the counting game.

The child needs to learn the rule that he or she stops after counting to a specifically given number

Repetition is important for children of this age. At bedtime and at other convenient times, the parents should spend a moment or two reviewing numbers. This should be done casually and almost incidentally as a means of providing enough drill and repetition for mastery. A great amount of practice will be very valuable at this age. Provide the review experience at every opportunity and give as much practice as the child is able to absorb without frustrating or pressuring him.

Repetition is important for boys and girls of this age; review numbers often

Counting to Thirty

As soon as the child has attained mastery of numbers up to 10, the parents should help him to count to 25 or 30. This can be done in somewhat the same manner as the numbers from one to 10 were taught. Teach a few numbers at a time, beginning with 11 and going on from there. The child should understand how these numbers fit with the others and that the same counting experience can be applied. Through repetition, practice, and teaching approximately five more numbers at a time, the child will soon be able to master the additional numbers.

Teach a few numbers at a time until the child can count to thirty

Learning Number Symbols

Only after we know that a child can count to at least 10 and only after we are certain that he understands that the sound symbol made with the vocal cords represents a number, will we be ready to teach written number symbols. Parents should think about the sound symbols made with the voice and the written symbols of the numbers. The child has often learned that the sound made with the vocal cords for the number three represents that number. He knows that this sound means something, and he knows what it means. It is then a simple matter to teach that the written number "3" is merely another means of communicating the basic idea of three.

At a particular moment when the child is interested and it appears that his attention span is right, the written number symbols can be presented. The parent should explain certain distinguishing characteristics of each number. Use some of the same techniques utilized in teaching the letters of the alphabet in chapter 9. Do not present too many concepts at a time, and use opportunities to repeat when the child is interested and when you have his attention.

Teach the written numbers as you taught the letters of the alphabet

Using TV Shows and Toy Libraries

The written symbols for numbers are interestingly presented in "Sesame Street" and other TV shows. Parents may want to use this means for follow-up, tutorial sessions with the child. Games in the toy libraries that teach written number identification should also be used at this time. They have been designed to supplement and enrich the instruction of this book, and they provide definite and concrete experiences, using two or three of the senses. Our purpose in teaching numbers and number symbols is to have the child become thoroughly familiar with numbers zero (0) through 10 and to have him able to recite the numbers from one to 30.

As you play number games with your child, try to help him do the following:

(1) Make sure that he is capable of number recitation from one to 30. This simply means that he can recite the numbers in consecutive order and is able to count from one to 30 flawlessly. In addition, his number recitation skill should make it possible for you to give him a starting point among these numbers, and he should be able to count from the number you give him to any given higher number that you might ask him to identify. For example, if you gave the child the number three and told him to count to eight, he would be able to count from three to eight by naming number four and going on, stopping at number eight.

(2) The child should have number matching skill. When you give him a printed numeral, the child should be able to select an identical numeral or number from a set or group of printed numbers. The toy library will help you in working toward this skill.

(3) The child should have number recognition skill. When you give him the verbal label or symbol for a number, the child should be able to select the appropriate number from a set of printed numerals. For example, when you say the number four, the child should be able to go to a set of printed numbers and select

Use television programs as follow-up in teaching numbers

The child should be able to count to thirty from any given number

The number matching skill should have been acquired by now

The child should have number recognition skill

"4" from this set. You may want to give him drill and practice in this by devising some interesting games where he will be successful most of the time and where you can give him some praise for his accomplishments.

(4) The child should have number labeling skill. This is the opposite skill from number recognition. It means that when you give the child a printed numeral, he will be able to look at it and give the verbal label or say what the printed numeral is; for example, you hand him the number "6" or you point to the printed number "6" and he is able to say "six."

The child should be able to look at a number and recite its name

Through numerous games and repetitious exposure to concepts, the child should have these skills well mastered. Our objective will be for him to reach this capacity by the time he is four years of age. (Some children may take longer than this, and parents should adapt to the child's level of interest at the time without undue concern if a few extra months are required to reach this capability.)

Another skill should also be mastered: The child should be able to enumerate. When he is given a set or subset of up to 10 objects, he should be able to count them and then tell how many there are. For example, if you pour seven blocks from a box onto the living room floor and ask him to tell you how many blocks there are, he should be able to count them and come up with the number seven. This requires him to be able to recognize that the last number reached in his counting is the total number in the set of objects. Your suggestions should be "Count the blocks. How many are there?"

The child should be able to count items you have placed before him or her

Although it is not essential, parents should also try to teach some additional counting skills. For example, when you arrange a group of objects in a circle, the child should be able to identify the first object that he counts by marking it or moving it out of the circle so that when he finishes counting, he will know that he has counted all of the objects. The same strategy can be used when counting a group of objects in a stack by teaching him to pick them up and place them, one at a time, in another stack.

The child must also develop the ability to recognize quality in numbers. He should be able to associate a group of four objects as equaling the number four. He should be able to match a group of five objects with an equal number or grouping of identical objects. Through practice in games, he should attain the concept of equality.

Quality in numbers should be known to the child at this time

Teaching Visual Discrimination

In preparing the child to have all the skills that will make learning to read less difficult, you must keep in mind that it is very important for the child to learn to recognize objects that are almost the same except for one or two subtle differences. In working with the simple geometric shapes, parents should draw triangles, circles, and squares with slight deviations in them. The child should be taught to recognize quickly that one of the geometric shapes has a slight difference in it.

Parents must train their child to recognize subtle differences in objects

A child should be given exercises in finding objects in a picture. Since he has learned the parts of the body, he should look at pictures of mothers and fathers, boys and girls and point out such details as nose, ears, knee, and so forth. He should be taught to look for expressions on people's faces on a picture page that may depict happiness, anger, crying, etc.

Children of this age should be able to recognize parts of the body in pictures

Parents should strive to help the child pick up information quickly with his eyes. Practice at this time in his life will give him an extremely valuable skill. Such practice does not always need to be in formal teaching situations. Opportunities (in the grocery store or while traveling in the automobile or walking in the neighborhood) will arise when the child can be taught to look for details that will help him to build visual discrimination power. If the parent has this objective in mind, numerous opportunities will arise to develop this skill in the child without much effort or pressure on him. It is a skill that can be acquired almost incidentally if parents are alert to use valuable teaching situations.

Parents should be alert to find valuable teaching situations to give their child practice in picking up information with the eyes

Building Additional Auditory Discrimination Skills

Earlier in this book we suggested activities, including use of toy library items, to build skill in auditory discrimination. As the child approaches four years of age, the parents should provide additional experiences that will help to build this important skill as a prelude to reading instruction. The parents should devise games that will help the child to copy rhythmic patterns. Children of this age love rhythm, and they will respond readily to rhythms and beats that have a pattern to them. For example, rhythmic patterns can be taught by the parent speaking or singing a pattern to be repeated by the child. Following is an example:

Children of this age love rhythm

The parent will say:
"Da da, dot dot, da."
This is said in rhythm with the "da" sounds spaced out long and the "dot" sounds spoken very quickly — one rapidly after the other. (This is done similarly to telegraphic codes of dots and dashes, where the dots are rapidly transmitted and the dashes are more slowly given.)

Other rhythm patterns such as the following can be given for the child to repeat:

(1) Dot dot dot dot, da da. (Say the fours "dots" rapidly and the two "das" slowly.) You may need to repeat this pattern several times at first.

(2) Da da da, dot dot, da. (Say the three "das" slowly, the two "dots" rapidly, and the last "da" slowly.)

Any number of similar patterns will give the child practice in hearing and giving back rhythmic patterns. The parent may also want to invite the child to give the rhythmic pattern for the parent to repeat back to the child.

The child should also be taught to rhyme words. This simple exercise can be carried out by giving the child two or more words and stimulating him to select or supply a third rhyming word. This activity may be associated with the rhythmic activities described above.

Describing the Properties of Objects

Before the child reaches the age of four, he should also have some experience in describing what educators call the *properties* of objects. Properties are the distinguishing characteristics of an object. (Several toys in most toy libraries will help the parent to teach

The ability to describe the properties of objects should have been acquired by now

this skill.) For example, the child should be able to look at several different triangles cut from plastic or wood. He should then be able to give the object's color and describe its relative size as compared to a number of other triangles that may be larger or smaller. He should also be able to examine its thickness and distinguish this characteristic from other triangular-shaped objects presented to him.

The child should have experience in describing the properties of other things with which he comes into contact. This may range from objects of wearing apparel to different dogs and cats in the neighborhood that may be alike but different in some respects.

Following is an example of the child's description of a ball that he has just examined as compared to another ball that he owns:

> The new ball is red and my ball is blue. The new ball is softer because I can press it in easier with my hands. The new ball bounces higher. The new ball will go flat because it is filled with air. My old ball is more solid, and it is not filled with air. The new ball has triangles on it, and my old ball has stars and circles on it.

The child should be able to describe objects and then to make comparisons to things that are familiar

The child should be taught to describe all of the properties that can identify a particular object, and make comparisons with other objects familiar to him.

As the child practices building this capability, he will also have an opportunity to continue to build his vocabulary. He needs to be able to express himself, and he needs to be able to observe and describe what he observes with a considerable amount of accuracy. By building the skill to distinguish between different objects and to describe the properties of them, he will develop a number of capabilities that will be useful to him throughout his entire lifetime of learning.

Practical Application

These examples are merely a foundation. Do not feel that all of them must be introduced at the same time or that they must be presented in the sequence given below. You should develop additional, more individualized activities for your child.

Yesterday, Today, and Tomorrow

The following activities will aid your child in understanding what is going to happen each day and throughout the week so that he can anticipate his daily routine.

1. After reading steps 2 through 6, make a pocket chart with seven slots for inserting cards or pictures which will represent the days of the week to your child.

2. Determine some routine event for one day of the week only (such as attending church, shopping, or other activities) which involves your child.

3. When you are going about these activities, take a picture or draw one that includes him.

4. Place each picture showing an event in one slot of the chart; for example, going to church on Sunday, shopping on Friday, etc.

5. As explained in the text of this chapter, repeatedly help your child understand the concept of yesterday, today, and tomorrow.

6. You can also make a toy clock to hang on the wall and attach pictures that represent routine events for each day. Include such activities as getting dressed in the morning and breakfast, playing, eating lunch, taking a nap, daddy coming home, dinner, and getting ready for bed.

Fun with Numbers

To help your child learn written number symbols, incorporate the following methods in your teaching techniques:

Make a pocket chart with seven slots for pictures which will represent days of the week to the child.

Attach pictures (photos, clippings, or drawings) to a toy clock to represent routine daily events.

The toy clock is useful in teaching time concepts, numbers, and in encouraging the child to converse.

Allow sufficient time for the child to learn each number. Help him to understand what each means.

Show the child two shapes in sequence. Mix them up and have him put them back in the same order.

Teach him to reproduce the shapes with a pencil or finger paint. Encourage him to start at the left.

1. Smooth some finger paint on paper. Take your child's finger and guide it to make a number. As the number is being drawn, say:

"Start up here and go down."

"This is number 1."

2. With you helping him, make the number at the top of the paper. Now make broken lines of the number (similar to follow-the-dot games) and have your child go over them to make a solid line. Constantly explain the features of the number as he works with it.

3. After he has mastered step 2, make just a portion of the number and have your child complete it.

4. Allow ample time for him to learn each number. As he learns to write the number, help him draw objects which represent it (four squares and the number "4" or two circles and the number "2").

5. Vary this activity by using glue and beans, glue and glitter, or play dough.

Look Carefully

1. Show your child two shapes in sequence (a triangle and a circle). Tell him to look at them carefully. Mix them up and have him put them back in the same order as you had them.

2. After he has mastered the task with two shapes, increase the number to three. Remember to make this a successful experience, and do not move the activity along too quickly.

3. When he is able to place the shapes in the exact order, show him the shapes once more and then mix them again. Now have him reproduce the shapes in sequence using finger paint or paper and pencil.

4. Remember to encourage your child to start at the left and move to the right when studying or reproducing the sequence of the shapes.

How Do I Feel?

At this age, your child has an increased awareness of his facial expressions. He enjoys looking at himself in a mirror and contorting his face to reflect various emotions that he now recognizes. The following activity, though it may seem unsophisticated, can cement a good relationship between you and your child if he realizes you have seen him "pull faces" secretly and that you approve.

1. Assume a sad appearance and say:

"This is my sad face."

"Look at my eyes and lips."

"Now you make a sad face."

2. When your child is able to identify and make the various expressions, make two different facial expressions (sad and happy) and then have him repeat them. Present three different expressions and have him repeat them in the same sequence.

"This is my sad face." Playtime activities help build vocabulary and encourage free communication.

Tell Me

Provide the following opportunities for your child to express his descriptive abilities. Use this experience as an opportunity to introduce new concepts and vocabulary. Work together to discover everything about each object.

1. Choose a topic that includes nursery rhymes, stories, personal experiences, etc. Say:

"Tell me about [name the story]."

Provide opportunities for the child to express her descriptive abilities with words and gestures.

2. Make an obvious error when counting (when he knows the numbers) or when reciting nursery rhymes, stories, or other topics in which you can include some nonsense.

"My dog said 'meow.'"

"This is the story of Jack and the cornstalk."

3. Have many objects before your child and ask him such things as:

"Tell me some of the things that are the same about these."

"Tell me some of the things that are different about these."

Arrange objects before the child and say: "Tell me some things that are the same about these."

Help the child appreciate the phenomena of nature, with attention to details such as flower petals.

Visit places where men and women are working, and begin to introduce your child to the world of work.

Getting to Know You

1. Arrange to visit a senior citizen center where your child can talk with someone from the older generation. (Be sure to call in advance so that your visit is convenient to their schedule.) This can be a very rewarding experience!

2. While at the library, look through the publication *Occupational Outlook Handbook.* Jot down the description of some interesting careers and locate firms and businesses where you and your child can watch men and women at work. Choose occupations that will not only be interesting to your child but to you as well. By reading the *Handbook,* you will be more prepared to ask questions and be familiar with the occupation.

3. With your child, explore the phenomena of nature. Show him a caterpillar inching its way along a branch or icicles forming on the eaves of the house or on a bush. Show him small details such as the bark on trees, small insects, seeds, the petals of a flower, etc.

11 Additional Learning for Three- and Four-Year-Olds

Not only should the child three to four years of age be able to recognize the letters of the alphabet, he should develop the ability to recite the alphabet from *A* through *Z*. He should also be able to recite the remainder of the alphabet when given a particular letter; for example, if his parents give the letter *O*, the child should be able to continue, in consecutive order, the remaining letters in the alphabet to *Z*.

The three- to four-year-old child should be able to recite the alphabet

Additional Skill Building in Learning Letters

In addition to alphabet recitation skill, the child should also have more practice and drill so that he can flawlessly do the following:

(1) The child should have letter matching skills. When given a printed letter, he should be able to select an identical letter from a set of printed letters set before him.

The child should have letter matching, recognition, and labeling skills

(2) The child should have letter recognition skills. When he gets the verbal label for a letter, he should be able to select the appropriate letter from a set of printed letters; for example, if he is given the letter *Q*, he should be able to go to a group of letters and select a *Q*. This should be done after the parent repeats the letter "Q" verbally.

(3) The child should have letter labeling skills. When he is given a printed letter, the child

should be able to look at it and verbally give the name of the letter; for example, when handed the letter *K*, he should be able to look at the letter and say, "This is *K*."

Teaching Elementary Phonics

Phonetic sounds of the alphabet should be started

Some children, before the age of four, will be ready to learn the phonetic sounds of the consonants. They may also be ready to learn the long vowel sounds (the sounds of the vowels that "say" their own names — *a, e, i, o, u*).

After the child has mastered the letter recognition, letter labeling, and letter matching skills described above, he is ready to begin to learn a few elementary phonetic sounds. These should be taught very casually, with games devised to make fun out of learning. It is easy for parents to press too hard in teaching phonetic skills. The light-handed, casual touch is recommended. Teach in an incidental and off-hand way as you talk, play, and work with the child in his daily routine.

The parent should begin teaching the sounds that letters make by explaining to the child that, in addition to a letter having a name, it also makes a sound. (Later, the parent may want to explain that some letters make more than one sound — as shown by the TV "pop up" shows.)

Parents should not teach words at this time, only letters and sounds

Parents should *not teach words* at this time, but merely repeat the consonants (*b, c, d, f, g,* etc.) and have the child learn through practice and drill and through continuous games to give not only the name of the letter but the sound it makes. Although the long vowel sounds are easily taught — since these letters say their own names — they can be taught more easily and casually after the sounds of the consonants have been mastered by the child.

Make sure that each sound is produced properly

Make sure that each sound is produced properly. Pay special attention to the fact that some letter sounds are spoken and some are whispered. For example, the sounds for *F* and *S* are whispered sounds. However, *L, M, N,* and *R* require voice sounds. Games and drills through use of books and toys will help to motivate the child to learn while he acquires his first phonetic skills.

Caution in Teaching Phonetic Skills

Some children will acquire phonetic skills readily, while others may have a difficult struggle. Parents should delay teaching these skills if the child encounters problems. The emphasis should be on the casual and almost incidental teaching of some phonetic skills as you play with your child. It is not essential that the child master these rudiments of phonetics by the age of four if he needs a few more months to be ready. Avoid pressure, but teach as you live and play with your child in your home.

Parents should delay teaching phonetics if their child has problems learning this skill

Keep in mind that our program is an ambitious one and that the child is receiving many stimulating learning activities. Be careful not to press too hard. Permit your child to move along at a natural speed for him.

Additional Strategies in Teaching Phonetic Sounds

As you teach the child the sounds of letters, you will find yourself using vowel sounds with consonants; for example, *B* has the sound of "bee." The strategy is to teach the child to drop the final vowel sound. Make the sound and teach him that the sound is "bbb." In like manner, when you give the name for *D*, you say "dee," but when you teach the sound for this consonant, say "ddd." The same applies to such letters as *T, V, J, K,* and others.

The vowel and consonant sounds can be taught

In teaching the sounds of letters such as *F, L, M, N, R,* and *S,* remember that the name of each letter starts with a vowel sound and ends with a consonant sound. For example, *F* is pronounced "eff" and *L* is "ell." You pronounce *S* as if it were "ess." In teaching the sounds of these letters, teach the child to drop the vowel sound and merely say the sound that is left when the vowel is omitted. Practice this several times and be ready to help the child avoid confusion when you teach these fundamental phonetic concepts. (Be sure you understand these concepts as you teach.)

The child should be taught that there is a group of letters which make more than one sound. Tell him that the letter *C* sometimes has a "sss" sound (as in the word "cent") and that *G* sometimes sounds like "jjj" (as in the word "gentle"). Tell him that these letters and others sometimes make different sounds, but do not spend too much time explaining this be-

Simple drill on the various sounds of "c" and "g" can be touched on at this point

cause he will learn them later and should not be confused at this time. (The only purpose in mentioning these exceptions to him here is to prepare him for subsequent instruction so that he will not be bewildered but will remember later in his learning experiences that exceptions were mentioned to him.)

Conversations between Parent and Child

The parents should encourage conversation by the child

Research on learning has taught educators to recognize the value of response and action in learning. The parents should encourage the child to be responsive and to participate through action and through initiation of activity. Many simple facts and many mind-stretching experiences can emerge from an alertness to learn vocabulary, conversational skills, and thinking processes all at once. The child should be taught his name and address. He should know the name of his parents. He should learn concepts such as brother, sister, mother, father, husband, wife, aunt, uncle, grandmother, grandfather, son, daughter, grandson, granddaughter, and cousin. All of these relationships to people will be helpful to the child in stimulating his vocabulary, his thought processes, and his conversational skill. Parents should keep a steady flow of conversation that adds facts and enriches the body of knowledge for the child.

Teach your child his or her name and address

Summary

The child who has been exposed to the full range of learning experiences recommended in this book (to age four) will have had an opportunity to grow intellectually far beyond that of the typical child of this age. These experiences should greatly enhance his intelligence and his ability to learn.

These experiences should greatly enhance the child's intelligence and ability to learn

We have emphasized a number of times that learning should be fun, and have placed considerable emphasis upon learning through creative play. We have cautioned against pressure and emphasized the need for successful experience and for wide application of the reinforcement theory. We have stressed the necessity for adjusting the level of difficulty to the capacity of the child and again emphasized that the child, through his responses, should indicate to the parent how to adjust the teaching and learning program.

We have emphasized that individual differences and variations in the growth cycles of children make it impossible to recommend a standard of performance applicable to all children. Therefore, we have attempted to recommend those tasks and outline those learning skills that will meet the needs and match the capabilities of the typical child. The parents should make adaptations and adjustments. This should be a simple task for the parents — since no other two human beings should know a child more intimately or have more interest in his intellectual growth and educational maturation than the father and mother.

The parents should make adaptations and adjustments as they teach

Children love to play and interact with others. This program of early childhood education assumes that play can be creative and that learning can be a game. Therefore learning and play can be one if the parent judiciously uses the natural inclinations of the child for this purpose.

As we conclude the fourth year in our program of early childhood education, let us recommend that the parents review some of the fundamental principles of teaching and learning for the preschool child. Assess your experiences to this point with your child, keeping in mind that you have another excellent year before the child is ready for kindergarten and formal schooling. Be prepared to make the most of this final year in your program of home-based, early childhood education.

Assess your experiences to this point with your child

Practical Application

These examples are merely a foundation. Do not feel that all of them must be introduced at the same time or that they must be presented in the sequence given below. You should develop additional, more individualized activities for your child.

Find time to include all members of the family in teaching discussions to provide added motivation.

Use rewards and positive reinforcement in order to increase interest and give additional incentive.

Learning can occur at any time. During or after a family meal, play a guessing game with sounds.

What's My Name?

The activities outlined below could be separated into two groups, one for the three-year-old and the other for the four-year-old. If your child has learned his name by the time he is three, you may want to omit the first four steps and teach him steps 5 and 6. (At this age, it is imperative that children know their names because they are old enough to play outside the home and could easily become lost.)

1. Have different family members say to the child:

> "My name is Sally and your name is Tom."

2. After he is familiar enough with the sounds of the names, say only your name and let the child finish the sentence:

> "My name is Sally and your name is ...."

3. Reverse the procedure by saying:

> "Your name is Tom and my name is ...."

4. While sitting around the breakfast or dinner table, have one family member tap his glass or make some other sound and ask:

> "Who made that sound?"

Take turns in guessing and making sounds.

5. After your child has learned his given name, teach him his surname. Explain to him that all members of your family have that name added to their other names.

6. If your family surname is difficult for him to pronounce, cut it up into syllables and teach it to him as short words . . . Evanovich can become "Ee-von-oh-vitch," or Hendriksson can be pronounced "Hen-drick-sun." Do not laugh at his attempts to conquer multi-syllable names.

Sounds Are Different!

Learning the sounds of the letters of the alphabet can become tedious to a child. Teach no more than he is willing to learn at one time. The following activities should aid the parent in teaching the child how to pronounce letters.

1. Have your child feel his throat (larynx) when sounding the letters *L*, *R*, *G*, and *D*, and his nose when saying *N* and *M*. Point out the vibration he feels.

Have the child feel her throat when sounding some letters. Point out the vibration that she feels.

2. Use a mirror to show him the position of the lips, tongue, and teeth when he is making such sounds as "vvv," "fff," "bbb," "ttt," and "ddd."

3. Place three cups upside down on a table, and put a chocolate chip, a marshmallow, or another edible item under one cup. Explain to your child:

> "I am going to make three sounds, and one of them will be 'fff.' When you hear the 'fff' sound, pick up the cup that I am pointing to. If you are right, you will find a chocolate chip under it."

4. Point to the first cup and say:

> "Bbb. Is that the 'fff' sound?"

If the child responds with a "no," point to the next cup and say:

> "Fff. Is that the 'fff' sound?"

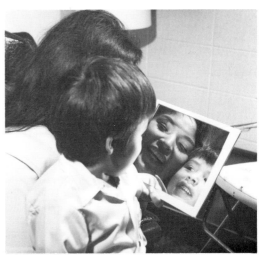

Use a mirror to show the position of the lips, the tongue, and the teeth when making frontal sounds.

"When you hear the ' ff ' sound, pick up the cup I point to. If you're right, you'll find a cookie."

Instruct the child that you are going to make the sound of a letter and he is to color that letter.

Show the child the numbers on your home, apartment, or mailbox to help him understand about addresses.

Have the child help you address letters to others, and show the child letters you have received which correspond with the numbers of your home address.

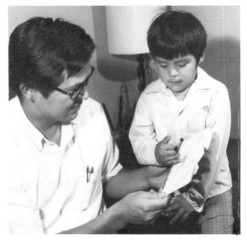

If he says or even nods a "yes," say to him:

> "Pick up that cup and see if
> the chocolate chip is under it.
> If it is, you are right."

Color the Sound

1. After your child has learned the sound association with a letter, copy several different letters on a sheet of paper.

2. Instruct your child that you are going to make the sound of a letter and that he is to color that particular letter on the paper.

3. When your child has mastered the association between the letter and the sound, you may want to present two different sounds and have him color them. This will increase his auditory memory and general listening skills.

My Address

1. To assist your child in comprehending the meaning of the word "address," show him the numbers on your home or apartment building and the numbers on other buildings on your street.

2. Have him help you address envelopes to other people, and show him mail you have received which corresponds with the numbers he has seen on your home.

3. If there are four digits in your home address, teach him the first two by

placing them in front of him. Add the third number and coach him until he can say the first three numbers in their proper sequence. Add the fourth number and repeat the process. Continue this task until you feel your child has thoroughly grasped the concept.

4. Scramble the four numbers and ask him to put them in their correct positions.

5. Engage in a review activity by asking him to reply to your questions:

"Do you live on Maple Street?"

"No."

"Do you live on Pine Drive?"

"Yes."

"Is your house number 4837?"

"No."

"Is your house number 4832?"

"Yes."

Teach the numbers of your address by presenting one number at a time. Use play numbers or cutouts.

When the child learns the address, review it often Scramble the numbers and have her reorder them.

12 Learning during Four to Five Years

By the time your child is four years old, he will have reached a level of capacity and performance that will make it possible for him to learn at a very rapid rate, particularly if you have worked with him through the earlier months of his life and if you have presented most of the stimulating and nurturing experiences described in this book.

With the proper background for learning, the child will be able to learn rapidly

Characteristics of the Four-Year-Old

The four-year-old is very independent and, if he is typical, will also be a bit defiant of parental instructions. By the time he has reached this age, he can converse rapidly. He will have picked up some "earthy" language if he has been permitted to play with older children who use profanity. He will also be prone to express his frustrations and to blame his parents for his own mistakes.

The four-year-old is independent and and bit defiant, with flights of fanciful imagination

Most four-year-old children have very unusual flights of imagination. Studies of early childhood development describe the four-year-old as a "teller of lies." Since most four-year-olds enjoy fiction more than fact, they enjoy telling of things created purely from their imagination.

When the child is four, it is time to begin a pattern of slightly stronger direction and to teach reasonable rules of behavior. The exuberance of the four-year-old must be controlled, at least to a limited extent, and most parents find they must exert a sub-

The parents should begin a slightly stronger set of rules of behavior

stantial amount of firmness. The four-year-old should be given opportunities to test his abilities and to expand his limits of exploration out-of-doors and around the neighborhood. This will provide an outlet for the aggressiveness typical of this age.

Studies of child development and child personality growth indicate that in the early years of life, most human beings experience extremes of behavior, typified by insecurity and rebelliousness and followed by periods of obedience and a strong desire to please. These fluctuations in behavior seem to be nature's way of helping the child develop and expand his capabilities. As he gets older, these extremes of behavior diminish to a more even pattern representative of an attitude of accepting life and the rules of living.

By the time the child reaches 4½ years of age, he will have moved into another phase of behavior that will be less volatile and challenging to the parent. The child at this age is improving in his control and in his ability to cooperate and participate in family affairs. He is highly motivated toward conversation and will want to discuss many things with his parents. This is especially true if he is on easy terms with his father and mother. The child will be full of questions and anxious to receive explanations.

Watching for Fears and Apprehensions

Many children, during the age from four to five years, develop fears and concerns that need attention from parents. It is not unusual for children at this age to have nightmares and cry out in the night. Some children under stress bite their fingernails and urinate in moments of emotional excitement.

All in all, this period from four to five years of age will prove to be a challengeng time for parents involved in home-based, early childhood education programs. It is a time for parents to be thoughtfully concerned about helping the child develop good habits of cooperation and participation in family life. It is a time for firmness mixed with loving understanding.

Children constantly need parental love, but the four- to five-year-old is in particular need of the security and assurance that he is loved by his parents. Review your relationship with your child. Show some extra affection and concern at this time. Love is a

Children this age experience extremes of behavior: from insecurity to obedience

The child of four is able to control herself or himself, and will cooperate and participate in family affairs

Many children develop fears that need attention from the parents

It is time for a certain amount of firmness mixed with loving understanding

powerful force in teaching and learning . . . use its power to advantage.

Vocabulary Development for the Four-Year-Old

During the time that a child is four to five years old, parents should strive to develop his vocabulary as rapidly as possible. Research indicates that between the ages of two and five years, a child adds approximately 500 to 600 new words each year to his vocabulary, indicating the great receptiveness that preschool children have for learning. During this final year before the child enters school, you will want to use this receptive power to help him build a rich vocabulary.

The four-year-old is particularly fascinated by words. He is learning to express ideas and feelings through use of a vocabulary. At age four, most children have learned to talk quite clearly. Four-year-olds are avid conversationalists, and parents should use this great interest and desire to converse to maximum advantage. Throughout this book, we have attempted to emphasize the great value in stimulating vocabulary development. At no period in the child's life is this more important than from the ages of four to five.

Along with his vocabulary development, parents should be conscious of helping a child to enunciate properly. Be sure to speak clearly and simply to your child. Do all that you can to help him speak in complete sentences. Encourage him to express himself clearly, but to do so by using complete sentences.

Age four is a time of great natural curiosity. Parents should use this to maximum advantage in building vocabulary and understanding of the world surrounding the child. Be sure to continue to expand his contact with books, and do all possible to help him have satisfying experiences with them so that he will have a good outlook and attitude toward them.

Parents will find the four-year-old full of questions. There will likely be times when the child will ask more questions than the parent may consider reasonable. Be sure that you are not impatient with this questioning. It is part of his great curiosity, and you should be doing what you can to cultivate an attitude of wanting to know rather than discouraging him by refusing to answer or ignoring his questions. Be sure to respond and make explanations to questions

The parents should strive to develop their child's vocabulary as rapidly as possible

The four-year-old is fascinated by words and can talk quite clearly

Be sure to speak clearly and simply to your child

Age four is a time of great natural curiosity

Parents will find the four-year-old full of questions

as simply and directly as possible. Your behavior should encourage mind-stretching conversation. Keep the conversation flowing.

The child at this age will be particularly anxious to have multisensory learning experiences. He will explore through touching, tasting, smelling, hearing, and seeing. Be sure to encourage this and expose him to all of the senses as a means of bringing his mind into contact with the real world around him. Most parents underestimate the capability of four-year-old children. The child at this age is much more capable of absorbing information than many parents realize. Be sure to help your child take maximum advantage of this time in his life when he will be eager to learn and will be filled with curiosity and enthusiasm.

The child of this age is anxious to explore through touching, tasting, smelling, hearing, and seeing

Attaining Social Maturity through Play with Others

Most children will be entering the formal school structure shortly after they turn four. It is therefore important that parents pay particular attention to the social maturity of the child. Give your child as many opportunities as possible to meet other children of the same age. Provide opportunities for sharing, playing, and working together with others. This will help the child make a better adjustment to school life. It will help him develop wholesome attitudes toward, and have respect for the rights and feelings of others.

Give your child as many opportunities as possible to meet other children of the same age

Teaching Reading to the Four-Year-Old

When the child is four years old, parents should encourage him to review the letters of the alphabet and to practice drawing the letters with a pencil or crayon. He will develop some hand-eye coordination and control as he traces or tries to form a rough approximation of letters. Use the letters in the toy library so that the child can coordinate his senses of sight and touch in working with letters.

Your child will develop hand-eye coordination with drill in writing numbers and letters

Have him repeat the names of the letters as you say them so that his sense of hearing can also make impact upon his mind. Through these multisensory experiences, he will reinforce the knowledge he has and will be able to apply it as he builds upon this background. Parents should continue to teach and to review, through practice, the sounds the letters symbolize. (You may want to reread the material in previous chapters to make sure that your child has a solid background in this area.)

After the child has completed a good review of the letters of the alphabet and understands some of the basic sounds of the letters, he is ready to be exposed to a few simple words and to learn that the alphabet is the building material for words and that written words are useful in his life. The formal and systematic teaching of reading is a job for professionally trained teachers. In this book it is suggested that a few word recognition experiences be provided. Some children will want more word recognition experience, and others should wait for further maturation. Help your child to see words as symbols for objects with which he is familiar. Do this casually, but do not try to teach by formal instruction.

Expose the child to a few simple words; teach him that the alphabet is the building material for words

When the child's interest is high in some simple object or in some possession of interest to him, take the opportunity to form a simple three- or four-letter word. Show him the letters and remind him of the sounds for them. Through this, you can present to him for the first time the idea that a group of letters stands for something. For example, if the child has a cat or dog in which he has a great interest, you may, at an appropriate time, introduce him to the word "cat" or "dog." This can be followed by pictures that may have captions identifying the objects.

Casual Exposure to Printed Words

In introducing the child to his first experience in reading, be very casual about it. Present the concepts as incidentally and naturally as possible. Slip an idea in here and there in your daily experiences with him. This is a good time to print some simple cards and label a few of the common objects around the home. Put the word "bed" where he sleeps at night. In a casual way, show him the word and remind him of the letters that he has already learned which make up that word, and also remind him that the word represents the name of the thing he sleeps in at night. Do the same with other objects, such as the toys he plays with, the eating utensils he uses, and so forth. This is all part of creating a responsive environment around the home to expose the child to ideas in a very casual and natural way, free from pressure but full

Create a responsive environment in the home so that your child will casually pick up the meaning of written words

of rich and meaningful experiences at any time the child is ready to absorb a new concept.

Parents should be extremely cautious to teach these few, simple, introductory, word-meaning ideas in a manner that will avoid any possibility of the child's developing an adverse attitude toward reading. Remember that it is important to teach, casually and almost incidentally, a few simple words at a time. (Do not demand or insist in any way that a word be learned. Simply expose the child to the word and let him absorb what he will from casual contact. His formal teaching will come at school.)

Coordination with Television Programs

The lessons on word exposure and preparation for reading in such TV programs as "Sesame Street" and the "pop up" intermissions in cartoons will supplement the casual approach of introducing reading to the child during the four- to five-year-old period. Follow up the TV lessons with some relaxing play, with the child using the subject matter that was presented. Words commonly used in television word recognition drills are as follows:

big	love	stop
bird	me	street
bus	mop	telephone
danger	pat	the
exit	pet	up
fun	ran	us
I	school	walk
is	sit	you
let	spot	

The parents should create word lists that are labels of familiar objects in the home

Parents should develop their own word lists that are labels for common objects found around the home and familiar to the child. Keep word cards on the objects and refer to them often when working and playing with the child.

Play word matching games with your child

Another word recognition skill is to help your child match a printed word on a card with an identical word from a set of printed words. Let him practice this, but help him by giving clues. Try to make a game of it while remaining casual and relaxed. Remember that his *attitude* and *outlook* toward the entire matter of reading is more important than his merely learning a word.

You may want to expose the child to some decoding skills as shown on TV programs. For example, you may want to teach him to recognize and point to the first and last letters in a word. Words, to a child just learning to read, are strange symbols that, he is told, have meaning. He must learn to pronounce a printed word when he sees it. He needs to learn how to use certain clues to help him know what the word is. By looking at the consonants and vowels and by thinking of the sounds that they make, he will have some clues to help him. By looking at a word he knows, such as "man," he can learn to recognize the word "ran" simply by substituting the letter and sound of "r" for the letter and sound of "m."

The child must learn to pronounce a printed word when he sees it

Later, as he advances to where it will be useful, you can even show him how to recognize the first and last words in a printed sentence. This may also be done from a book while you read to him. Practice in decoding related words will help the child acquire a useful reading skill. In addition, the child should be taught to recognize words in sentences. Help him during reading and story-telling times to find words that he has learned. (You should use the incidental approach and avoid any temptation to get into formal teaching.)

Drill in decoding related words will help the child acquire a useful reading skill

The child should be taught to recognize printed words in a sentence by realizing that the space between words indicates where one word ends and another begins. Practice this element of learning with him. The test will be when he can look at a sentence and point to each word in it. He should also be taught that all reading moves from left to right. This is usually learned incidentally, but parents should be careful to point it out and make sure that the child understands this concept.

Teach that the space between words shows where one word ends and another begins

The ability of four- to five-year-old children to learn a few simple reading skills will vary considerably from one child to another. Parents should continue to teach, using the play and game approach. We cannot overemphasize the importance of attitude and outlook toward reading. Parents will help the child immeasurably by teaching through the incidental and casual approach that reading is fun. The child is not mature enough to have a rigid situation thrust upon him or to receive reading instruction as it is taught

We cannot over-emphasize the importance of attitude and outlook toward reading

in school. We are seeking exposure, using the home as a responsive environment for teaching through the casual method.

Some children, by the time they reach the age of five, will have a reading vocabulary in excess of 500 words. Others may not respond at all but will be ready a few months later. The important thing is to follow the dictates or mood of the child and avoid all pressure. A vocabulary of 500 reading words is exceptional, and parents should accept whatever can be attained from a program of instruction described in this book.

The best strategy for parents to follow in reading instruction is one of casual exposure, following the systematic teaching of the alphabet recognition skills described in the previous chapters. If the child responds with great interest and quickness in reading words (using the letter recognition and sound decoding skills), be alert to take advantage of the readiness and learning ability that he displays. If, however, the response is somewhat confused, the parents should use the "soft sell" approach, avoiding pressure and teaching according to the response of the child. By implanting seeds of interest, the parent can make progress without negative reaction.

By implanting seeds of interest, the parent can make progress without negative reaction

Making Sure Your Child Is Ready for Reading Instruction in School

You will note from the foregoing discussion that a formalized and systematic approach to teaching reading is not recommended at this time. Our purpose is to prepare the child for formal reading instruction and to expose him to opportunities to begin reading if his aptitude and progress are such that he is ready. With the type of background information and alphabet recognition skills presented in our pre-reading program, your child should enter school with skills and capabilities far exceeding that of the typical kindergarten child.

A formalized and systematic approach to teaching reading is not recommended at this time

Systematic and formalized reading instruction should be left to professionally trained teachers. We should avoid conufsing the child with a varied approach. We have thus limited our effort to attaining certain pre-reading goals and to teaching word recognition, decoding, word matching, and casual exposure to a few limited words.

Avoid confusing the child with a varied and competitive approach

If a gifted or talented child is ready to learn to read, the parent will be able to recognize this. We recommend that each child be encouraged to move along as far and as fast as he desires. A few children will actually be reading from these experiences. However, the typical child will only be able to master the pre-reading goals and attain the skills that we recommend as being valuable to him as he enters school.

The child should be encouraged to move along as far and as fast as the child desires

Teaching Relational Concepts

During the 12-month period from four to five years of age, parents should strive to give the child a solid understanding of a number of relational concepts. The mastery of these will provide mind-stretching experiences as well as basic skills that will be useful in school.

Through the use of educational toys and other teaching opportunities in the home and neighborhood, the parent should strive to help the child understand such concepts as "same" and "different." In addition, the child should learn to understand size relationships such as tall and short; big, bigger, and biggest; small, smaller, and smallest. He should be taught some quantitative relationships such as more, most, all, less, some, and none. This basic teaching in relational concepts should move on to include positional relationships such as up, down, beginning, end, first, next to, around, under, over, on, and through. The child should be taught distance relationships such as near, far, close to, and away from. Then he should be taught temporal relationships such as first, last, before, after, next, beginning, and end.

Teach relational concepts: big, bigger, biggest; same and different; tall and short, etc.

In teaching all of these relational concepts, the parent should use concrete illustrations as much as possible. For example, in teaching the size relationships of big, bigger, and biggest, the parent should use actual objects to demonstrate. Understanding the meanings of these words will be much easier for the child if this is done. Positional relationships — under, over, above, and below — can easily be taught.

Use actual objects to illustrate the concepts

It is important that the parent strive to lead the child's mind to complete mastery of these concepts. The mind-stretching experiences of mastering these concepts and the benefits derived therefrom will be most useful in school.

Practical Application

These examples are merely a foundation. Do not feel that all of them must be introduced at the same time or that they must be presented in the sequence given below. You should develop additional, more individualized activities for your child.

Explain that many things are different yet alike. You can draw with a pencil, a pen, or a crayon.

Teach the concept of relative size by showing the child objects that are "big, bigger, and biggest."

Print a number of different letters on a sheet of paper and ask the child to circle one letter.

Name Something Like It

1. Explain to your child that many things are different yet alike. For example, you can draw with a pencil, but you can also draw with a crayon, a marker, a brush, a pen, etc.

2. Select categories fairly familiar to your child and name other objects which have something in common. For example, take turns naming objects similar to a shoe (boot, slipper), knife, bed, car, fruit, vegetable, etc.

3. Expand his vocabulary by introducing unfamiliar objects which are part of a particular category . . . hem, sleeve, pocket, buttonhole, zipper, etc. (dress), wheel, spoke, handlebar, etc. (a tricycle).

Roll the Dough

Play dough (recipe in chapter 4) can provide the means by which relational concepts can be taught.

1. With your child, use the play dough to demonstrate the relational concepts discussed in the text of this chapter. Make three different-sized balls (small, smaller, smallest). Put one ball on top of another (top, bottom; on, off). Put one ball near and one ball far away, etc.

2. After your child has acquired the knowledge of several basic concepts, take him outdoors and ask him to point to such things as the big, bigger, and biggest tree; something that is near, far, next to, under, over, etc.

Color the Letters

1. Print or trace several different letters on a sheet of paper.

2. Instruct your child to color all the *M*s red, the *E*s blue, etc.

3. To incorporate a counting exercise, you might indicate the number of times a letter appears by saying:

> "The letter *M* appears seven times."

> "Can you find all of them?"

Complete the Letter

1. Make a portion of a letter either with paper and pencil or with crayon, finger paint, beans, or other objects.

2. Have your child complete the letter. It may be necessary that you make a model for him to follow.

3. Point out the characteristics of each letter to aid your child in acquiring knowledge about letters.

Make a portion of a letter or a dotted line of a letter and ask the child to complete the outline.

Opposites

This activity can increase your child's vocabulary if you take the time to demonstrate the concepts that are unfamiliar to him.

1. Instruct him that you are going to say a word and have him say the opposite, such as:

> "This cloth is wet."

If he doesn't respond "dry," show him two cloths — one wet and one dry.

2. Place a book on a chair and another under the chair. Say:

> "I'm putting this book *on* the chair, and this book *under* the chair."

Have him repeat the activity for you, explaining to you as he does it.

Let's Act It Out

1. Dramatize nursery rhymes, favorite stories, or daily activities.

2. Encourage conversation with one another as the "play" is enacted.

3. In addition to using this activity for vocabulary building, use it to display various feelings of emotion, reactions, and change in tone and emphasis of voice quality.

Increase the child's vocabulary by teaching him to distinguish between such qualities as wet and dry.

Take the time to demonstrate concepts that may be unfamiliar; i.e., *under* the table and *on* the table.

13 Additional Learning for Four- and Five-Year-Olds

This chapter is for four- to five-year-olds who have mastered the contents of the previous chapters but need an additional challenge. It offers abstract reasoning and problem-solving experiences for children who have demonstrated complete mastery of the curriculum content of this book. Parents are advised to review the progress of the child and spend additional time on this chapter only if it is apparent that the child is ready to proceed with the learning experiences that follow.

Developing Reasoning Power through Classification Practice

The child should be given opportunities to work with groups of objects, to sort them out according to various types of classification. He should, for example, practice classifying objects according to their size. He should then have groups of objects that he can classify according to their functions or the purpose for which they are used. When presented with a group of geometric shapes, he should be able to classify them according to their forms as well as to other aspects such as color, thickness, etc.

A typical exercise in classification practice is to give a child a can filled with nails, screws, nuts, bolts, and washers. He first arranges the objects into five groups. He then puts the finishing nails (those with very small heads) in one pile and the box nails (those with larger, flat heads) in another pile. He then classi-

Children this age should be able to classify objects and groups of objects as to color, size, thickness, etc.

fies and sorts them further by size. He may even be taught to classify them for outside use (those that are galvanized) and for inside use. He goes on to do the same with the screws, nuts, bolts, and washers. This experience helps him to organize and to make decisions according to what he can see and how he can reason about the functions and properties of the objects.

The child should know the functions of objects

An additional exercise to develop this ability should be presented to the child by having a number of like objects, except for one. The child is then stimulated "to reason" as he approaches the question: "Which of these things belong, and which do not?" Several items of wearing apparel and one object such as a spoon or dish will provide a basic experience in this regard. (The child should be able to see that the object used for eating does not belong in the group.) As he practices this, he should be given more complex groups of objects to identify and classify.

The child should then have practice in classifying objects on the basis of more than one characteristic. He should be able to see a group of geometric shapes and classify them by color, size, shape, and thickness. The complexity increases as he learns to identify, for example, a group of triangles that are yellow and of the same size and thickness. Other sorting and classifying experiences can easily be created by the parent through use of materials in the toy library and other items around the home.

Learning Experiences in Arithmetic for Four- to Five-Year-Olds

Possibly no other subject area in the school curriculum causes more children to feel inadequate and instills a dislike for learning as much as mathematics. Since arithmetic is such a systematic and logical subject, it lends itself to organization and arrangement into regular instructional sequences. Therefore, learning arithmetic can be made easy for the child if care is exercised in observing the response of the learner and adjusting the level of difficulty to his needs.

Learning arithmetic can be made easy for a child if care is used to adjust the level of difficulty to the child

The fundamental precept of adjusting the level of difficulty (to a point where approximately 80 percent of the responses are correct) should indeed apply in the teaching of arithmetic. Children should be success oriented in arithmetic with even more care than in any other subject area. The most frequent mistake of a parent is to eagerly press the child into levels of difficulty far beyond his capability, causing needless stress that makes arithmetic seem difficult to him.

As you stimulate the child's mind to casually attain a few basic mathematical understandings, be careful not to move too rapidly. Resolve to help the child to have a wholesome experience so that he will be positive in his attitudes and will begin with the impression that arithmetic is fun.

Help the child have wholesome experiences so he will have a positive attitude toward learning

Strategy of Teaching

At this point you should review the level of attainment of your four-year-old. Go over the material in chapter 10 and make sure that your child has attained the counting skills and learned the recommended number symbols. Review the specific skill capabilities outlined in chapter 10 and patiently work with your child on them before proceeding to the recommended material that follows.

Teaching Addition and Subtraction

You can teach addition and subtraction as you work and play with your child around the home if you will be conscious of opportunities to stimulate his thinking about numbers. In placing knives, forks, and spoons on the table as you prepare a meal, be sure to involve your child in the activity. Ask him to add two additional spoons and then get him to tell you the total number. Follow this by indicating that three spoons plus two spoons equal five. Use concrete illustrations such as this. Let the child have manipulative experiences that will help him think arithmetically. He will soon get the idea that simple addition is the same as counting and that simple subtraction is just counting backward or in reverse. By having the casual approach used on him, he will learn addition and subtraction without being aware of his efforts.

You can teach addition and subtraction as you work and play with your child

Place objects on the living room floor when you have playtime with your child. As you enjoy games together, devise ways for him to solve some simple subtraction problems. If, for example, you are playing with 10 blocks, spread them out in an orderly fashion on the floor and follow through the logic of conclud-

As you enjoy games together, devise ways for him or her to solve simple subtraction problems

ing how many blocks you have after you subtract three from the total group. Go over a number of subtraction combinations in this way to provide the child with a broad range of experience in thinking numerically as he works and plays.

Most educational toy libraries have various kinds of devices that will illustrate to children the logical implications of adding and subtracting. Be sure to avail yourself of the opportunity of using some of these toys in giving further enriching experiences to your child. Read the instructions carefully and be particularly aware of the need for the child to have approximately 80 percent successful response from his experiences with these toys. Adjust the level of difficulty so that he will feel successful and will have a "can do" attitude.

After you have determined (through play experiences) that he has the skill to solve simple addition and subtraction problems, you may want to begin to teach him, through continuing practice with printed cards, games in which he can quickly solve simple addition and subtraction. Some children at this age are ready for this type of learning by reading printed

Teach addition and subtraction symbols

numerals which have addition or subtraction signs ("+" or "—"), and they will respond immediately after thinking through the solution. You should offer this opportunity only if the child has been successful in the previous experiences of working with addition and subtraction problems by counting certain objects. Keep in mind that it is much more difficult for him to read one number and then another and mentally arrive at an answer to a problem.

You must help him bridge the gap of *merely counting* objects and then adding or subtracting and being

Help your child to bridge the gap between merely counting and adding or subtracting

able to *understand the written numerals* and then adding or subtracting. Do not press your child to obtain the latter skill unless he has done well in the previous activity and unless he is obviously enjoying the stimulation. Remember to apply the 80 percent success response principle here, making sure that you adjust the level of difficulty so that eight out of 10 responses are correct. This method is extremely important in teaching arithmetic, particularly for the preschool child.

Watching for Teaching Moments outside the Home

You should be watching for opportunities to stimulate the thinking processes of the child in experiences outside the home. Watch for numbers and other items on road signs as you travel in your car. Help him realize that we are surrounded with mathematics in our daily lives. Teach him in a manner so subtle that he will be learning arithmetic without realizing he is doing so. In this way, his skills and mental capacities will grow naturally. This experience will be particularly pleasing for him if you are clever in your approaches and if you keep the level of difficulty adjusted to his unique circumstances.

> Help the child to realize that we are surrounded with mathematics in our daily lives

As you look at magazines, books, and illustrated materials, watch for opportunities to teach arithmetic. Show him such things as a mother animal with her offspring or a train with cars attached. Opportunities will abound for the casual, incidental, and very natural method of arithmetic instruction we advocate in this book if you are aware that yours is the responsibility to stimulate the mind of your child with these subtle approaches. Many of these kinds of natural experiences will provide the readiness for a more formal use of arithmetic with written number symbols.

> Opportunities will abound for casual, incidental, and natural methods of teaching arithmetic

For some children, the challenge of learning from lists of written addition and subtraction problems may be appropriate at this time. Such formal practice sessions will not by any means be the proper approach for every child. You should, however, progress to such activities if your child is showing high promise and great interest. Let the child's response tell you what to do. Most of all, be very careful not to generate negative attitudes or create a failure complex. Keep in mind that there is plenty of time and that it is not essential that your child master simple addition and subtraction at this age. Teach with love, care, and optimistic recognition and reinforcement for whatever progress the child is ready to achieve.

> Be careful not to generative negative attitudes or create a failure complex

Learning to Reason through Arithmetic

Because mathematics is almost pure logic, our purpose in early childhood education is not only to teach valuable skills that can be used in school but to develop the cognitive powers of the child and help him to build a more powerful intelligence. When a child is four years of age, the parents should create experiences for the child to think about problems and to mentally project outcomes and solutions.

In your daily play and work activity with your four-year-old child, try to follow his thought processes. Particularly in the area of arithmetic, be alert to diagnose what his problems are if he is having difficulty. Strive to be sensitive to your child and as aware as possible of his thinking processes by talking about how he arrives at solutions to problems and challenges you give him. If you are keenly aware of your child's learning difficulties, you may get a valuable clue that you can use as a key to helping him over a hurdle in learning.

Be sensitive to your child and as aware as possible to his or her thought processes

Using Several Senses in Teaching

Be particularly careful to use a multisensory approach in teaching. This can easily be done in teaching arithmetic, especially with children who are having difficulty in learning. Many experts recommend, for example, the use of plastic or paper numbers. The child's tactile sense can be used as an input to his mind if he gets the "feel" of numbers as well as being able to see and hear you speak the names of the numbers. Use this approach to adding another dimension to learning if your child is having difficulty. He will enjoy cutting out paper numbers and pasting them on squares if you approach it as a part of your daily playtime.

Use a multisensory approach in teaching; have your child use all of the five basic senses

After he has created his plastic or paper numbers (some toy libraries have sandpaper or felt numbers), you can add to the tactile experience by having him place a number of objects beside the actual numeral. For example, three buttons could be placed on the floor under the plastic numeral three. The child who is having number and arithmetic difficulties could, in this way, use his sense of touch and his actual manipulative ability to give further input into his mind as a means of reaching an understanding about quantities represented by the numeral symbols.

To help the child build his ability to reason and use logic in problem solving, give him experiences in creating problems for you to solve. Have him present number equations to you by placing on a table or the floor a group of three buttons and then (spaced a short distance away) a group of four buttons. Let

Let your child give you problems to solve

him ask you how many there would be if you combined the two groups. Your response would then demonstrate through analysis of the two separate quantities and through counting procedures how you arrive at the correct answer.

Additional Experiences for Advanced Children

For children who apparently demonstrate great interest and considerable aptitude in arithmetic, parents should move on to teaching equations. Such equations can be written on paper with a blank to be filled in. For example, you may want to give the child practice in addition problems where the answer is supplied but one of the key numerals is missing. By writing $6 + \quad = 9$, you introduce the child to simple equations that will be stimulating if he enjoys this particular type of exercise. You may want to go on where three numbers are added to equal a larger number. For example, you could present an equation such as: $3 + 2 + \quad = 9$. (The child would then be stimulated to supply the answer of the number "4" in filling out the blank number.)

If the child has mastered number concepts, give him simple equations to solve

Such experiences with equations can even be demonstrated with objects on the living room floor. Merely substitute a number of objects for the written numeral symbol and have the child pick up the number of objects and insert them in the blank space in the equation. Such experiences are particularly useful for children who have aptitude and interest. Most four-year-old children will likely not be ready for such an experience at this particular time. In keeping with our desire to help every child attain his full potential and advance as far as he can when ready, these suggestions on equations are presented in this book as an enrichment activity.

Group Games in Arithmetic

For those homes in neighborhoods where children can play and learn together, some group games using arithmetic to develop logic to solve problems can be devised. For example, a game of baseball could be played wherein children advance around the three bases by responding correctly to arithmetic problems. Three errors on a side would be three "outs," and the other side would come to bat. Obviously, parents

Simple games that involve arithmetic can be devised for your child

sponsoring these types of group activities will need to adjust the level of difficulty to the abilities of the children. It will require some insight to recognize that some children are not ready for advanced problems but will have to be given a problem equal to that particular child's ability to answer.

Many other games can be developed, limited only by the imagination of parents and children. Since children love to play and enjoy group activities with others, it is wise to take advantage of this natural inclination to provide another opportunity for the child to learn naturally and incidentally as he enjoys his association with others.

Teaching the Concept of "Zero"

In teaching arithmetic reasoning, parents may want to introduce and teach the meaning of "zero." Strange as this may seem to adults, young children seem to have a particularly difficult time understanding what zero means. It is hard to teach that it means "nothing" because you cannot demonstrate it as easily as showing that three buttons or three blocks represent the numerical symbol three.

Although the concept of "zero" is hard for the child to understand, it can be taught

As you work in your counting and number games with your child, you may want to place a number of buttons or marbles in some pans or dishes on the floor. While doing this, try putting one empty dish out. Show your child this dish (after he has counted and answered your questions concerning the number of objects in the other dishes) and ask him to tell you how many buttons are in this dish. When he replies that there "aren't any," use this particular opportunity to explain that "zero" means "none" or "nothing."

Some children have difficulty in understanding that $6 + 0 = 6$. This can be illustrated in a more concrete manner by having six buttons in one plate and no buttons in another. You can then illustrate that the six buttons in the one dish and zero buttons in the other equal a total of six. The same type of demonstration can be used in teaching subtraction where zero is involved. By using such demonstrating opportunities, you can teach this simple but often difficult concept.

Give the child opportunities to develop problems and equations using addition, subtraction, and zero in the thinking and answering processes. Parents should take care to change roles so that the child has the pleasure of developing questions and providing the leadership in some of the games. He will be more motivated to learn if he has an opportunity to be the leader once in a while. This will also give him the chance to think and to formulate in his mind some questions and equations. Give him an opportunity to participate in this way and help to provide all of the variety you possibly can.

Parents should often change roles with the child so the child can do the asking

Review and Practice in Arithmetic Skills

It is important to review frequently the number concepts that the child has mastered. Remember that this can be done while riding in the car or when he is outside the home with you in the grocery store or around the neighborhood. Use these opportunities also to help him review as well as learn new concepts. Until these basic skills are firmly rooted in the mind of the child, he will need constant opportunity to use his abilities and exercise his mental processes insofar as mathematical reasoning is concerned. Give him ample opportunity to practice and demonstrate what he has learned, and be sure to praise him and to recognize his accomplishments.

Use every opportunity to review the arithmetic skills of your child

Teaching the Days, Weeks, and Months

In chapter 10, we suggested that you introduce your child to the concept of time. After he has had considerable experience in arithmetic reasoning, he should be ready to learn more about how we record time and the terminology we use in telling days, weeks, and months. Since the child has some ability with numbers, he will now be able to look at a calendar and be given some instructions on how we record and keep track of our days.

Teach your child how to record and keep track of time

Help your child understand that time is valuable. Talk to him about the life span of different living things. Explain to him the length of time that most human beings live. Explain the expected lifetime of his favorite pet. Through use of an encyclopedia, you may be able to get some valuable information that will be useful in describing how time is measured. You may also be able to get some information that

Tell your child about the life span of living things

will be useful to you in explaining the life expectancy of different animals.

After you have had opportunities several times to have incidental conversation on the concept of time, teach your child that a day is made up of the period of daylight when he is awake and the period of time at night when all of the family are asleep. Explain that a new day has been born each time he wakes up in the morning. You may want to explain how the sun furnishes light. (The solar system is too complex to explain at this time.)

The important concept to get across is for him to understand what a day is. Be sure to take as much time as necessary in this explanation. Over a period of several days, you may want to talk to him about it and call his attention to the fact that it is early morning, midday, afternoon, evening, time to go to bed, and then time to get up in the morning to begin another day.

Through a conversational approach to this over a period of time, the child will soon get an understanding of what we mean when we talk about a day. He should then receive some explanation that will help him understand that there are seven days in a

Explain the concept of time: day and night; weeks; months

week. Help him to be conscious of the fact that we begin a new week on a particular day, and through the activities of the home, we go through a routine in a week, culminated by a weekend and the beginning of another time period that is somewhat repetitious of the previous one.

If he has not previously learned them, teach him the names of the days of the week and help him through practice and drill to be able to name them in proper consecutive order. You may want to help him become familiar with certain things that are unique to your home that have to do with work that is accomplished on a particular day of the week. All of this will help him gain a concept about time.

Teach your child the days of the week

After the child understands the concept of days and weeks, teach him through use of a calendar to understand the concept of a month. Show him that there are 12 months in a year. Explain the seasons of the year and call his attention to the fact that in his short lifetime there have been changes in the weather and in the climate outside that have affected his life and the routine activities of the home. Although it is not essential to do so, you may want to help him learn to repeat in consecutive order the names of the 12 months. You should not spend too much time on this because in the mind of a child, a month is indeed a long time. He has not experienced very many of these periods of time in his short lifetime. The important thing is for him to begin to get the concept about time and how it is measured.

Teaching How to Tell Time

Teaching children of this age to tell time by the clock is difficult. It will be useful, however, to teach the child to recognize the hours and tell what the approximate hour is by identifying the number to which the small hand on the clock is pointing. Since he now has an understanding of number concepts and can read numbers, this will not be a particularly difficult thing to do.

It will be useful for the child to know something about telling time by clock or watch

It is somewhat difficult for a child to understand how the large hand on a clock functions in indicating time. He must be able to count by fives and to grasp a number of abstract principles before the full ability of telling time will come to him. It is recommended

The child should
understand the
value of telling
time

that the child understand the value of telling time and attain the ability of telling the approximate hour by looking at the face of the clock. (This can be done by your calling his attention to the fact that the small hand is the hour hand.) However, with the exception of children with extremely high interest and considerable ability, teaching the actual skill of telling time should be delayed until after the child has entered school.

Teaching Measurements and Measuring

Another useful and beneficial activity applying some of the skills learned in arithmetic is to help the child understand and apply various measurements that we use around the home. Since all measurements are quantitative and involve the use of numbers, this is a natural follow-up activity that will broaden the concepts and basic understandings of the child, at the same time giving him additional opportunities to apply what he has learned.

Show your child
how distances
are measured

Begin your activity of exposing the child to the concept of measurement by showing him how distances are measured. Through the use of a ruler or a yardstick, show him how to measure the length of an object that is familiar to him. If you are measuring the length of the kitchen table, for example, point out the numbers and introduce him to the terms of "inch" and "foot." Show him how you can mark the space for one foot or one inch with a pencil, and help him understand that what he has learned about numbers will be useful in this type of activity. You may want to follow this by measuring his height on the wall, using a yardstick, ruler, or tape measure. Give him many concrete experiences in the use of linear measurement.

Introduce the
child to the
measurement of
volume

Next, you should introduce your child to measurement of volume. Most household kitchens have ample devices, and the parent has numerous opportunities to do this. Let him participate in following a recipe from your cookbook. By doing this, he could learn the numbers in your book that indicate certain measurements, and you could help him grasp the idea that another measurement similar to linear measurement is the measurement of volume in terms of ounces, pints, quarts, gallons, and so forth. You may want to give him a problem where he would measure a given quantity of water through application of the knowledge that you presented him.

Your child is also ready to learn about the measurement of weight. If you have a bathroom scales, let him weigh himself and also weigh other objects around the home. Help him realize that this is another important measurement used in our everyday lives. He can apply more of his arithmetic ability through actual experiences that you can plan for him, and he can broaden his understanding and extend his vocabulary at the same time.

The child is also ready to learn about the measurement of weight

Teach measurements gradually and incidentally as the occasion presents itself in the home. Be alert for opportunities to remind the child that we live in a world where numbers and quantity are important. If it is convenient and useful, you may want to introduce him to the concept of the units that make up our money system. This can be done by showing him various coins and demonstrating how many coins of different value it will take to make a dollar. All such activities will broaden the experience and extend the depth of understanding of your child. Expose him to as many measurements and experiences in becoming familiar with quantities and with the application of numbers and arithmetic as possible.

Teaching the values of coins can be fun

Value of Incidental Teaching

The importance of incidental teaching and casual instruction as it emerges from the natural situation of living in the home and neighborhood cannot be over-emphasized. As contrasted to formal and disciplined learning experiences, the casual, incidental method takes advantage of practical teaching moments and eliminates the necessity for discipline and formal study. In teaching measurements and the application of arithmetic skill around the home, the natural, incidental approach will be productive only if the parent is consciously alert to seize upon opportunities.

Casual, incidental teaching as opposed to institutionalized instruction is most important to the child's learning

Practical Application

These examples are merely a foundation. Do not feel that all of them must be introduced at the same time or that they must be presented in the sequence given below. You should develop additional, more individualized activities for your child.

Give the child practice in classifying objects as to size, weight, use, color, or even ownership.

Show how four rocks on one side of the pencil and one rock on the other side "add" up to five rocks.

Show the child how coins relate to one another in value and point out how much various items cost.

Add or Take Away

1. Place a number in front of your child. Below the number, have a pile of large beans (or something comparable) and a long pencil.

2. Place the pencil so that the point is facing the number.

3. Using the beans, assist your child in putting different amounts on either side of the pencil to illustrate the combinations which will equal the written number.

4. For example, if the number "5" is used, you would place one bean on the left side of the pencil and four beans on the right side while explaining to your child. Then the beans could be moved so that two beans are on the left and three are on the right, etc.

5. Repeat this activity to show the addition and subtraction combinations for each number. Be sure to allow plenty of time for each combination so that your child will comprehend the relationship and meaning.

How Much Does It Cost?

1. Make a chart to display the value of various denominations of money. For example, using real money, glue a penny to a piece of paper and glue a piece of candy beside it. Then glue five pennies and a nickel and explain that both are equal in value, and glue a 5-cent item beside them. Demonstrate the value of the quarter, half-dollar, and dollar. In each instance, include how many pennies it takes to make a nickel, how many nickels it takes to make a dime, etc.

2. Set up a play store and have your child make purchases. This can be a lot of fun in addition to providing a learning experience.

3. Take the time when making real purchases in stores to point out how much an item costs, and have your child select the correct amount from the coins in your hand.

How Long Does It Live?

1. Pick several flowers that are in different stages of life — even dandelions will do — to demonstrate the life sequence . . . getting ready to bloom, full bloom, full seed, and dried up.

2. Guide your child's observations so that he can grasp the concept of time passing and the life span.

3. Have your child place each flower in the order described above to test his understanding of the concept.

4. Use other examples such as blossoms, leaves, plant size, root growth, etc. You may want to plant a seed and when it starts to break through the soil, plant another beside it. Keep repeating the planting until there is a sequence of five different growth levels.

Fill It Up, Please!

1. Use liquids (water) or solids (flour, sugar, sand) to teach the various measurements of volume, such as teaspoonful, tablespoonful, cupful, pint, quart, gallon, and so forth.

2. Demonstrate how many teaspoonfuls it takes to make a tablespoonful by counting as you dump one teaspoonful of sugar at a time into a tablespoon.

3. Take this opportunity to demonstrate that the same amount of water may fill one container which is tall and narrow, whereas it may barely cover the bottom of another container (vase and large bowl).

What Is Its Weight?

1. Begin by using two items of approximately the same size but extremely different in weight, such as a rock the

Pick several flowers in various stages of life to demonstrate the concepts of time and the life span.

Use liquids to teach the measurements of volume, such as a teaspoonful, cupful, pint, etc.

Take the opportunity to demonstrate how containers of different shapes relate with regard to volume.

Let the child feel the weight difference between two items which are approximately the same size.

child can lift and a ball of cotton. Have him hold one of the items in each hand to feel the difference.

2. Using the bathroom scales, show him that the indicator does not move when the cotton is placed on it, but that the rock makes the numbers on the scales move.

3. Have your child weigh himself. Then hand him his cat, puppy, or a fairly heavy toy. Have him watch what happens to the indicator when you take the object away from him. Write down the total weight and the weight without the object, and have him watch you figure the difference so that he can see how much his "puppy" weighs.

4. Have all the family members participate in the weight demonstration. Continually point out why one thing weighs more than another.

Have the child weigh himself; then show how the indicator changes when he is handed various items.

Continue to teach sound discrimination. Show how various objects make different sounds in a tin can.

14 Preparing Your Child for School

As the time approaches for your child to begin his formal schooling, it is important that steps be taken to make this adjustment as easy as possible on him. This chapter will outline some procedures that should be followed in preparing your child for school. It will also include some instructional activities to be carried out by the five-year-old in the home.

Make the adjustment to formal schooling as easy as possible on your child

Teaching Directions and Geographical Relationships

By the time he is ready to enter school, your child should be aware of the geographical relationship of his home to other places in the neighborhood. Moreover, he should have some information about the community in which he lives and how it relates to his neighborhood and home.

Help the child to gain an understanding of the location of your home in the neighborhood

Sometime after the child has reached 4½ years of age, begin talking to him about the neighborhood and the community in which you live. Help him find his way to places of interest in the neighborhood. Show him your house number, and teach him how streets are named and how houses are numbered. Help him to gain an understanding that certain places and specific homes can be located because they have addresses. Teach him your family address and help him be able to recall and repeat this without difficulty.

Explain to your child the concept of the four basic directions of north, south, east, and west. Explain that the sun comes up in the east and goes down in the

Explain east, west, north, and south to your child

west. Make sure that he understands that these are general geographical directions which will be important to him in finding his way in the community and in the neighborhood. Help him through repetition and incidental reminders to understand the four basic directions by identifying them with certain landmarks that can be recognized from his home.

Explain to your child that when he is facing east and puts his hand out to the left, he is pointing to the north. Explain that directly behind him is west and that by putting his hand out to the right, he will be pointing south. If your child has not learned to distinguish between his left and right hands, you may need to review this casually and incidentally over a period of days until he understands this concept.

Your child will learn that the directions of north, south, east, and west are constant. He should know that wherever he might be, the identification of these basic directions will be important to him. As you go to the neighborhood grocery store, take a few moments to point out the four basic directions so that he will understand that orientation of himself to these directions requires a different identification when he is outside his own home. Watch for opportunities to teach a sense of direction while your child is this young. As you travel with him in the car and as you move about the community, look for additional teaching moments when your conversation can lead to pointing out these important concepts to him.

Watch for opportunities to teach a sense of direction while your child is this young

Teaching Your Child to Walk to the Neighborhood Elementary School

If your neighborhood elementary school is within walking distance of your home and if your child will be required to walk to and from school, you should avail yourself of the few months before he enters school to teach him how to get there and to return home safely. Show him the best route to follow. Walk along with him to school and back several times. Point out some safe places to cross the street, and teach him awareness of traffic. Be sure to emphasize safety. Help him to become self-reliant and independent in this matter.

Show your child the best route to school

Small children often feel insecure in school if they are confused or if they have doubts in their minds about their ability to return home. It is particularly important that the small child enter school with full confidence that he can find his way home without any assistance if necessary. He will feel secure and will find himself confidently oriented if he attains this capability by the time he enters school.

Be sure to avail yourself of the opportunity to point out the four basic directions to the child while he is located at the school. From the school, you might also point out other places that are familiar to him, such as the neighborhood grocery store, the drugstore, the post office, and other places where you have often gone together. Do all that you can to make him feel properly oriented and secure in his surroundings at the school where he will soon be spending a large part of his time.

Help the child to be confidently oriented so that he or she can find the way home from school

Getting Acquainted with the School Building

After your child has become thoroughly familiar with the task of finding his way from your home to the school and back to your home, you should take a brief time to help him become familiar with the inside of the school building. From the viewpoint of the child, the school building is an enormous structure. He may feel frightened and lost inside it unless he becomes familiar with the internal surroundings. Some time spent on this will help your child feel more secure when he enrolls for the first time in the school.

Take your child to the school building

Walk around the school building with your child and point out the important places that he will soon be using in his formal educational experiences. Explain about the classrooms and how the corridors serve as "inside streets" in getting from one room to another. Explain the responsibilities of the school principal and the faculty members. Show your child the school lunch room and the rest rooms. Help him become familiar with the internal surroundings of the school building before school begins.

Explain about the classrooms and the corridors

Keep in mind that your child will be entering into a new world when school starts. He will be surrounded with friends and competitors in the classroom. He will have many social adjustments to make. If you have adequately oriented him to the physical features of the school and have helped him feel comfortable and familiar inside the school building, he will not have this added burden of adjusting in addition to the social adjustment that comes during the first days of school.

This emphasis upon the orientation to the school and upon finding a safe and secure pedestrian route from your residence to the school may seem to you to be unnecessary. Some children get along very well without this extra type of precaution and preparation. Many children, however, go through a sense of shock and frustration when they enter school. They cry and insist upon leaving for home in the middle of a school day. In extreme cases, they even resort to imaginary illness, bed wetting, and other avenues of psychological escape. Much of this can be avoided if parents systematically prepare the child for entering into the school system. Such orientation and preparation is another safeguard to make sure that the child is properly launched into his formal educational career and that the amount of adjustment and stress upon the child is kept to a minimum. He needs to feel secure and confident. This will be greatly enhanced if the parent takes the time to teach him.

Most schools welcome visits from future school pupils. If you find that you are welcome, take the opportunity to help your child get acquainted with the kindergarten teacher, the principal, and other individuals in the school. Keep in mind that the school is a very busy place and that most of the staff members are working under considerable pressure. Arrange your visits at a time that will be convenient for the school. Call in advance and adjust your situation to fit the circumstance of the staff members that you want to visit.

Teaching Games That Require Abstract Reasoning

During the summer months before school opens, your child should have an opportunity at this stage in his development to practice using his intellect to think ahead and project alternative outcomes from possible actions that he might take. He needs to be able to form in his mind what might happen if he does one thing as compared to what might happen if he elects to do another thing. Games such as tic-tac-toe, checkers, and simplified chess are excellent approaches to teaching these intellectual capabilities. After your child has passed the age of 4½ years, you should plan

---

Many children go through a sense of shock and frustration when they enter school

Most schools welcome visits from future school pupils

Help your child to think ahead and to project alternative outcomes

to introduce him to these three games and to teach him through creative play experiences to use his intellect in abstract, situational reasoning circumstances. Between the time your child is age 4½ and the opening of school, be sure to offer him numerous opportunities to match wits with you through use of these games. The following discussion of the three games may be useful to you in your teaching and learning experiences with your child.

Teaching Tic-tac-toe

As you introduce your child to tic-tac-toe, plan your strategy to attract his interest and to make sure that he has an enjoyable experience at the outset. It will take a number of weeks to lead your child to a place where he can play this game effectively. Whether he enjoys it and gains mind-nurturing experiences from it will be contingent upon how clever you are in making the experience a rewarding and reinforcing one for him. Be careful not to correct his errors in a way that damages the pleasure of the experience for him. Permit him to win and to have a successful experience, but do not make it obvious that you are being excessively charitable with him. As he learns, he will give you more competition, and the competitiveness can be more genuine. Play the game as often as the child's interest and initiative will permit.

As you play tic-tac-toe with your child, be sure he or she has an enjoyable experience

Teaching Your Child to Play Checkers

The game of checkers is a bit more complex than tic-tac-toe. Teach it after the child has learned the first game, or teach them alternately. You should explain to your child that he is now growing up and becoming quite powerful in using his mind. Try to introduce him to the game in a very casual way so that he will not feel compelled to play, but will have a curiosity and a desire to reach this level of competence and sophistication.

Try to introduce checkers in a casual way so the child will not feel compelled to play

Parents often have great success in teaching checkers by drawing on paper or cardboard a 16-square checkerboard. By using only two or three checkers on each side, the child is then confronted with a much more simplified approach to the game than would be the case with the full-sized checkerboard and the challenge of managing 12 men at a time. By using the

16-square checkerboard and two or three players, the parent and the child can experience the handling of the checkers and learn the rules of the game before using the more complex, full-sized game.

In teaching your child to play checkers, be sure that he has successful experiences. Let him make mistakes without very much instruction from your side. You may casually point out an error at the same time you indicate that you make errors in the game. It will be useful if you can discuss the game with him in a mature way wherein you can analyze the strategy and think through ways to improve. Remember that your purpose is to help project his thinking into future consequences of any actions he might take so that he will learn to envision an outcome of such actions and arrive at decisions based upon this ability to plan ahead in his mind the possible consequences. Let him learn by trial and error with some gentle suggestions from you. Be very careful not to "come on too strong" with instruction, correction, and finger pointing that will decrease his interest and pleasure. The game is for fun and intellectual development. Be sure that you work with him in such a way that he gains this from the experience he is having.

As you move to the larger game of checkers, be skilled in adjusting the level of competition so that he is challenged at the same time that he has successful experiences in winning and in capturing some of your men on the checkerboard.

Teaching Simplified Chess

Needless to say, chess is a highly complex game requiring an alert, analytical, and objective mind. It will be an excellent intellectual accomplishment for your child at this age to learn to play the simplified game of chess. If he has had successful experiences with the two previous games, he may be ready for simplified chess.

You may help your child want to play the game by explaining how "grown up" the game of chess is. You may show him newspaper articles written about chess and chess situations diagramed in the daily newspapers.

Casually teach the rules of the different players on the chess board. Practice different movements with

Be sure that your child has successful experiences from the game of checkers

Casually teach the rules of the players on the chess board

him so that he will understand the different movements of rooks, knights, bishops, and so forth. Gradually and systematically introduce him to this very fine game. Be casual and relaxed in your teaching strategy. Do not insist on playing chess unless he wants to. Then, when you do play, make sure that he has a successful experience and that he is permitted to quit when he desires. Watch his responses and adjust your teaching strategy to meet his needs.

It will be quite an outstanding accomplishment if your child at this age learns to play and enjoy the game of chess. Do not be eager to teach it if he has no interest — for learning chess is not essential. It will be, however, an avenue to further intellectual development if the two of you successfully learn to enjoy playing the game.

Additional Suggestions in Preparing for School

As the time for the opening of school approaches for your child, think through all of the preparations that will help to enhance his initial experiences at school. Check the condition of his health and make sure that he has had the proper immunizations and eye and dental examinations. You will want your child to be in good health and ready for the physical rigors of formal schooling.

Your child should be in good health and ready for the physical rigors of formal schooling

Help your child to be tolerant and understanding of others who may not have been as fortunate as he in receiving this program of instruction. Explain the need to be considerate of others. Help your child to anticipate with a positive outlook the new experience of entering school for the first time.

Practical Application

These examples are merely a foundation. Do not feel that all of them must be introduced at the same time or that they must be presented in the sequence given below. You should develop additional, more individualized activities for your child.

Encourage the child to express himself; question him about things he has seen or done during the day.

Use photographs or pictures to remind the child of familiar things and to help expand his vocabulary.

Play games such as tic-tac-toe, but use colored geometric shapes instead of the usual Xs and Os.

I Went to the . . .

To sustain a positive experience for your child during the following activities, stop before the sentences become so lengthy that he has difficulty adding items to the sentence.

1. Select different areas with which your child is familiar and say:

> "I went to the park and saw a tree. What did you see?"

Your child will respond:

> "I went to the park and saw some birds. What did you see?"

2. To extend this activity, repeat your sentence, but include his word or words, such as:

> "I went to the park and saw a tree and some birds. What did you see?"

3. After doing the activity in step 2, add another word:

> "I went to the park and saw a tree, some birds, and a swing."

Ask him to repeat your words, but add nother of his own.

Three in a Row

1. When playing tic-tac-toe with your child, use colored geometric shapes instead of Xs and Os to place in the squares.

2. Use this activity to review basic concepts previously learned by the child, such as geometric shapes, color, up and down, middle, left and right, etc.

I Live Here

1. With your child assisting, sketch an outline map of the immediate neighborhood, showing the position of his house in relation to streets and intersections.

2. Include such landmarks as the school he will be attending, the library, park, and other locations which will help him become oriented to his surroundings.

3. Take your child outside and show him streets and intersections. Point to the map each time you say the name of a street or building so that he will relate the map to the actual, physical thing he is seeing.

Where's the Other One?

The following activity will build your child's power of concentration when the cards you make in steps 1 through 3 are placed before him, upside down. You will be able to think of various other games in which you and he can use the cards.

1. Cut 16 two-inch squares from plain paper.

2. Line them up so that you have eight pairs.

3. With your child assisting, select eight identical pairs of pictures and paste them on the cards. (Identical pictures can be found in catalogs, stamp redemption books, newspapers, or on wrapping paper. If pictures are not available to you, draw your own, such as trees, dogs, etc.)

4. To start this game, use only three matching pairs and let your child mix the six cards (much the same as he would shuffle a deck of cards) and place them face (picture side) down in two rows on the table. Have the child randomly select one card and turn it over. After you both have seen the picture on it, have him turn it on its face again.

5. Now it is your turn to select and turn over a card, trying to match the one he chose. Let him see the card also. If it does not match, return it face down to its position. If your card matches the one he had turned, pick up both cards

Sketch an outline map of the neighborhood to show the child where streets and buildings are located.

Provide opportunities for the child to hear all kinds of sounds, including various types of music.

Make picture cards to play a mix and match game to help develop and discipline the youngster's memory.

and place them aside, and turn over another card for him to try to match. Help him to concentrate on the "tree" card that you or he had to replace so that when he turns up the matching "tree" card, he can say:

> "Oh, I remember where the other tree card is."

6. As your child becomes adept at matching three pairs, increase the difficulty by adding more and more pairs of cards to the "deck."

7. Use this activity also to increase his vocabulary and his sentence structure ability by repeating the names of the items on the cards and using each one in a sentence.

Picture cards and word cards can be used in many games and are very hepful in building vocabulary.

This educational toy kit was designed for use with preschool children from birth to age five years.

A Final Word

This manual has described an approach to home-based, early childhood education that teaches without formal, disciplined instruction. The program assumes that the child will increase his learning ability through absorbing what his parent teaches while at play, eating or dressing, helping around the house, or participating in regular family activities. The emphasis has been upon full use of those fleeting teaching moments that rise incidentally as the child interacts with his parents. The book has described techniques and emphasized procedures designed to keep the child constantly exposed to a stimulating, mind-nurturing environment.

The parent and child can build a lifetime relationship if this program is followed faithfully during the first five years of the child's life. The opportunities for observing and contributing to the intellectual growth of the child will create a bond of trust and experience sharing that will continue far beyond the age of five. Let the home become a child-centered place where the parents will be totally aware of the educational progress of the child through the developmental process of nurturing the infant's intelligence and preparing him for a promising school career.

As the parents learn to employ the reinforcement theory and as the reactions to learning efforts are observed, they will become very knowledgeable about the strengths and weaknesses of their child. They will become wise teachers as well as close companions to the child if this program is followed with true fidelity.

As parents, most of us want the finest opportunities for our children. In this aspiration, we often neglect the obvious need to make the home a learning laboratory and a supportive place for developing the attributes desired for a successful life. The home is the most powerful source of stimulation and motivation for the child. This program places the home squarely behind the child's long road to growth into full maturity through making an early commitment to develop the infant's intelligence. This strong commitment at the beginning of their child's life will reap untold dividends for the child and the parents throughout the entire lifetime of their child.

In terms of heritage and true environment for the child, there can be no gift of greater worth or lasting value than that of developing the latent talents of the child to full fruition. This is a gift within the reach of the most humble home with the most limited financial resources. The gift comes from the parents to the child through commitment to teaching as they live, work, and play together, and share many varied experiences. The gift comes from parents who care enough to take the time to provide truly creative play, mind-nurturing conversation, and experience-broadening activity in the home, neighborhood, and community. The gift comes from the parents who teach with loving concern and understanding, who realize that feelings and attitudes are of foremost importance. It comes from parents who observe reaction from the child and make wise adaptations to his needs. It comes from parents wise enough to teach a love of learning based upon successful experience from birth to age five and beyond.

Selected References and Additional Reading

Bloom, Benjamin. *Stability and Change in Human Characteristics*. New York: John Wiley and Sons, Inc., 1964.

Bruner, Jerome S. *Studies in Cognitive Growth*. New York: John Wiley and Sons, Inc., 1966.

——————. *Research Program on Intellectual Development*. Cambridge, Mass.: Harvard University Press, 1965.

Child Study Association of America. *Children of Poverty — Children of Affluence*. New York: Child Study Association Press, 1967.

Edwards, Esther P. *Wonder of Growing*. New York: Western Publishing Co., 1971.

Englemann, Siegfried and Therese. *Give Your Child a Superior Mind*. New York: Simon and Schuster, 1966.

Gesell Institute. *Child Behavior*. New York: Dell Books, Inc., 1962.

Hainstock, Elizabeth G. *Teaching Montesorri in the Home*. New York: Random House, 1968.

Hunt, J. McV. *Intelligence and Experience*. New York: The Ronald Press Co., 1961.

Jenkins, Gladys Gardner, *et al. These Are Your Children*. Glenview, Ill.: Scott, Foreman and Company, 1966.

Mussen, Paul Henry. *Child Development and Personality*. New York: Harper and Row Publishers, 1963.

Nimnicht, Glen, *et al. The New Nursery School*. New York: General Learning Corporation, 1971.

White, Burton L. *Human Infants: Experience and Psychological Development*. Englewood Cliffs, N.J.: Prentice Hall, Inc., 1971.

Index

YOUR CHILD'S INTELLECT: A Guide to Home-Based Preschool Education

The book is set in Baskerville and Helvetica. Paper is 80-pound Crown Matte from Zellerbach Paper Company. Composition was done by Paragon Press, Salt Lake City, Utah. Printing is two-color offset lithography, also done by Paragon Press. Binding was done by Mountain States Bindery, Salt Lake City, Utah.

DATE DUE

MY 2 '77			
JE 20'80			
GAYLORD			PRINTED IN U.S.A